The Little Book of Bob

James Bowen

HODDER

First published in Great Britain in 2018 by Hodder & Stoughton
An Hachette UK company

This paperback edition published in 2020

1

A CIP catalogue record for this title is
available from the British Library

Paperback ISBN 978 1 473 68853 7
eBook ISBN 978 1 473 68830 8

Typeset in Cochin by Hewer Text UK Ltd, Edinburgh
Printed and bound in Great Britain by Clays Ltd, Elcograf S.p.A.

Hodder & Stoughton Ltd
Carmelite House
50 Victoria Embankment
London EC4Y 0DZ

www.hodder.co.uk

To Ron Richardson, always there for me,
no matter what.

Very little is needed to make a happy life; it is all within yourself, in your way of thinking.

Marcus Aurelius

I have studied many philosophers and many cats. The wisdom of cats is infinitely superior.

Hippolyte Taine

Contents

Introduction

Like most people, I've made bad choices in my life. More than a few of them.

My decision to adopt a ginger street cat named Bob definitely wasn't one, however. Quite the opposite; I'd say it was the wisest move I've ever made. In many ways, we saved each other. He had been injured when I found him in the spring of 2007 and I'd nursed him back to health.

He certainly rescued me. When I look back on it, my life had been a real mess before I met him. For a decade or more, I'd been an addict and had spent an extended period homeless, sleeping rough or in shelters. I had been down to my last chance – on my ninth life, if you like. I credit him with helping me to turn things around.

I've often thought about the life Bob led before we met. To judge by the wounds on his body when I met him, he'd been living a precarious existence. He had obviously got himself into a few scrapes. But how had he lived from day to day? Had he always been a street cat? Or had someone else looked after him before me? I had no idea.

Throughout our time together he has remained a puzzle. An enigma.

One thing I have known from the very beginning, however, is that he possesses a wisdom that is unusual, even in cats.

I don't know if this has anything to do with lessons he learned during that earlier, mysterious life, but it's as if he is some ancient philosopher who understands everything and everyone around him. As if he's seen it all before. Knows life inside out.

Nothing seems to faze him. He takes every-thing in his stride.

In the decade since we met, he's grown even wiser, in my eyes. My life has changed quite dramatically during that time, thanks to a series of memoirs about our life together and then a movie, *A Street Cat Named Bob*. He has adapted to the changes that have occurred in our fortunes with ease. He is as comfortable meeting people at book sign-ings or film premieres as he was sitting on the pavement while I strummed my guitar in Covent Garden or sold *The Big Issue* outside the tube station at the Angel in north London.

I know it might sound strange or even slightly silly to say this about a cat, but I find him inspirational. Sometimes, simply sitting down and watching him is enough to set my mind whirring away. I'm fascinated by the way he conducts himself, the way he interacts with the world and responds to different situations. Even the way he lives his day-to-day routine. Being with him has opened my eyes to so much. Provoked so many thoughts. For the past ten years or more, he has genuinely been a kind of guru to me.

This book is a collection of some of the experiences and insights I've gained during my years with Bob. A guide to his street wisdom, if you like. I hope it helps you as much as he has helped me.

James Bowen
London, 2018

PART ONE

In Bob We Trust –
Lessons in Friendship

People often say that humans don't adopt cats; it's more a case of them adopting us. I suspect that is probably true. They are highly intelligent animals, after all. And deep down, I have a hunch they are smart enough to understand something that we humans too often overlook – the all-important value of friendship. I've certainly grown to appreciate it more – thanks to Bob.

Friendship Is a Pair of New Boots

Bob was a pretty rough-and-ready character when he came to live with me.

He didn't take kindly to being told off and could be a real handful if I stopped him from doing something. Before I had him neutered, he would lash out and scratch me. My hands bore the scars of his occasional tantrums.

I'd be lying if I said his behaviour didn't annoy me at times. But I had formed an instant affection for him and wanted our relationship to work.

At that time, I remember, I'd just bought myself a pair of black, army-style boots, from a local charity store. My old pair had literally fallen apart. The new pair did not quite fit me properly; the boots were a bit tight and had started to chafe and blister my feet. The best part of the day was taking them off.

It was as I slipped off the boots and let my feet breathe one evening, that it struck me.

Bob was pacing the flat, looking a little agitated. Earlier that evening, he had hissed at me when I'd tried to encourage him to use the litter tray I had brought into the house.

He was bound to feel uneasy with me and his new home, I thought to myself. Things I did were bound to rub him up the wrong way. But with patience, we would mould our friendship to fit each other's personality. We would get used to each other and our very different ways.

Our friendship was actually no different

to my new pair of boots. It was going to take time. There would be some discomfort. We'd irritate each other. But in the end, we'd fit each other just fine. And so it proved.

Free Spirits

The moment I knew Bob and I were destined to be together came, one unforgettable day, when he jumped on the bus to travel with me into London.

I had been flabbergasted. I'd shooed him away after he'd followed me to the bus stop from my flat and, as the bus had pulled away, had assumed he'd been left behind on the pavement. But suddenly, there he was, sitting on the seat next to me, curled up next to my guitar case as if he too was part of my luggage.

The bus conductor had smiled at me and asked me whether he was mine.

'I guess he must be,' I'd replied at the time, but I'd quickly come to realise that wasn't quite the case.

Bob is a force of nature, a free spirit. He wasn't mine. He wasn't a possession. I didn't own him then, nor do I own him now. We've chosen to be together in the present. But who knows whether we will be in the future? He will always be my friend, but he's free to leave whenever he wants.

I think that freedom is a key to any true friendship.

We Are All Stronger Together

I was cooking dinner one night, a few weeks after Bob and I got together. I was making spaghetti bolognese. Bob was curled up in the corner, watching me.

I'd put some music on the radio, boiled some water and was unwrapping the pack of dried spaghetti when the thought came to me. It was a distant memory from child-hood, of a fable or fairytale about an old man teaching his children a valuable lesson using a bundle of sticks.

'See this, Bob,' I said, snapping a single strand of spaghetti, before dropping it into the pan of boiling water on the hob.

'That's you and me before we were friends. When we were on our own.'

I then picked up a thick bunch of spaghetti, bending it one way then the other, but failing to break it in half.

'And that's you and me now.'

He tilted his head at me as if I was slightly mad. I wasn't, of course. I'd never said a wiser word.

Bob could have been spending that night out on the streets. Cold, lonely and hungry. Similarly, I could still have been living hand-to-mouth as a homeless addict. Without any focus or goal in my life. But the fact was, we weren't. We'd found each other. And we were better, safer and healthier for it.

We are all stronger together than we are apart.

The Truest of Friends

People are always fascinated by the special bond that exists between Bob and me. How did we come to form such strong ties? I've come to understand that the answer is quite simple.

We live in a world where it's hard to have faith in very much at all. Politicians, institutions, people – they all seem to let us down at one time or another. I certainly felt that way. A lot of my troubles were self-inflicted, but they were also rooted in broken relationships and the feeling that I'd been unloved.

Our relationships with our pets offer an alternative. We can rely on them. They don't lie to us. They don't cheat on us. They don't let us down. Their affection for us – call it love, if you like – is unconditional.

Knowing that friendship is always there for you is not only an immense comfort. It is a source of strength, too.

A Friend in Need

Everyone has fair-weather friends. They are present when the times are good. Always around to share in the celebrations, the parties, the easy stuff. But when – as inevitably happens – life enters choppier waters, these people melt into the background, or worse, disappear altogether. That's not a true friend. A true friend is there for you in times of need. When there's nothing to be gained. Or worse. Something to be lost.

There were times when Bob was totally independent, happy to be left to his own devices. He would sleep where he wanted, when he wanted. He explored my flat and the wider world as he pleased.

But he also had an ability to know when he was needed. I spotted it first when I picked up a bad cold, a few weeks after we'd got together. I'd been lying in bed, coughing and spluttering away, feeling pretty sorry for myself. I'd noticed him curled up close to me, just a few feet away from my face. He was purring away rhythmically. It immediately comforted me.

Apart from anything else, it made me feel like I wasn't alone. The purring was rather soothing, too. But there was something else, a sense of companionship, a feeling that was unusual for me – of my life being shared with someone else.

He has retained this habit. He's always attentive when I feel low. Instinctively, he seems to know when it is time for him to be a friend.

I've come to see that friendship is like this. It is not about being there every moment of the day – it's about being there when it matters.

The Same Path

It is much more difficult for someone to understand the journey you have under-taken if they haven't walked down the same

path as you. That's why the strongest friend-
ships are often forged in the same fire. The
tougher the times you've been through, the
tighter the ties that bind you.

That's certainly the case with Bob and
me.

We've been through so much together.
Bad times and good times. We have travelled
so far down that same road that our paths
rarely diverge. It's probably why, since meeting, we have never gone our separate ways.

True Friends Just Understand

We all have bad days. We all experience
times when, for whatever reason, everything seems out of sorts. The world seems
off-kilter.

Often you can't explain it. Nor do you
want to. You simply want to close the door

and forget about everyone and everything. Call it what you want: depression, the blues, a bad-hair day. It all amounts to the same thing.

At times like this, I've noticed that Bob's friendship is subtly different. Sometimes, I won't even be aware he is present. He will tuck himself under the chair or the bed, near me. On stand-by.

It's as if he's sensitive to my mood; as if he knows I need space, but that I also need watching. He seems to understand.

Again, I've come to see that's the mark of a true friend. They grasp instinctively that sometimes you don't want endless questions about what has upset you. You don't want to have to explain yourself. You just want someone to understand your mood – and nothing else.

Sometimes You Need to Lose Something to Appreciate It

A few years ago, I had to spend a period in hospital after developing DVT, deep vein thrombosis, a painful condition in my leg. I was still young, not even thirty at that point, but lying restlessly in bed for hours on end was a real wake-up call. It made me realise I'd taken my health for granted. I'd assumed that I was invincible, that I would always be fit and well, despite the obvious damage I'd done to myself as an addict living on the streets.

To my surprise, the absence of Bob hit me almost as hard. He had become my ever-present companion by that point. Always there to cheer me up.

As a result, I missed him really badly when I was in hospital. For obvious reasons, he couldn't come along and visit me.

When I was discharged, that first night back in my flat with him was as big a boost to my spirits as any doctor's diagnosis or any medicine they could have dispensed for me in the hospital. Any spell away from him now reminds me of that time, and reinforces my appreciation of how lucky I am to have him in my life.

Sometimes – as with your health – you have to lose someone's friendship in order to appreciate its true value.

Friends Can Be a Good Influence

Bob and I were on the London underground, heading home one evening. There must have been a football match going on, because the tube carriage was crowded with rowdy fans wearing scarves and shirts. We were squeezed next to a group of them

– four young lads – who were in pretty lively mood.

We had just pulled off from a station when one of them started chanting his team's name really loudly, within inches of me. His shouts caught Bob completely by surprise, but he dealt with it as most hard-bitten London commuters would. He arched his back briefly then turned away from them, nuzzling his head into my coat, as if switching off from the hubbub around him.

I hadn't had the greatest day and wasn't impressed by the lad's behaviour,

'Can you not do that. It's scaring my cat,' I said, as politely as I could.

The four lads looked bemused. They exchanged glances and then laughed. They probably couldn't believe they'd been ticked off by a man with a cat on his shoulder. But to be fair, they nodded at me as if in acknowledgment. They remained reasonably well-behaved until they got off the train, leaving me and Bob to ourselves.

A few years earlier, I would definitely have been more vocal. I might even have lost my temper. But tonight, I'd taken the view they were just young lads. They weren't doing any harm. I had bitten my tongue and let it go. I'd cut them some slack. I had a feeling I had Bob to thank for that.

He had helped me to see the world differently. Given me someone else to care for, someone else to think about. A responsibility that I hadn't really experienced before. And, perhaps without me even thinking about it, he had made me less self-centred. Kinder, more thoughtful, too.

Friends Are Free to Make Fools of Themselves

Every now and again, Bob will do something totally unpredictable. He might – for no apparent reason – decide to drape himself across the back of the sofa, stretching himself out in the most physically impossible position imaginable, seeming to defy the laws of gravity as he sleeps. Equally, he might suddenly start jumping and chasing around the room as if in pursuit of a fly or a wasp. His target is completely invisible – to me, at least.

If it were someone I didn't know well, I might worry. I might fret about the fact that he was acting out of character. That he's not the cat I once thought he was. But I don't. Because it's Bob, my best friend – I don't bat an eyelid.

I don't sit there analysing what has got into him, wondering whether there's some deep psychological issue. I watch and laugh. (Unless he's really doing damage to the furniture, of course.)

One of the great blessings of a strong friendship is that it gives you the freedom to be yourselves together, to let your hair down and go a little bit crazy every now and again. You know each other well enough not to take it seriously. It doesn't change anything long-term.

Share Your Good Fortune

To say that Bob transformed my fortunes is something of an understatement. In the ten years we've been together, my life has changed beyond all recognition. When we first teamed up, we had busked and sold *The Big Issue* together, living pretty much hand-to-mouth. In the past few years our job has been very different: appearing at public events and signings and on television to promote the books and the movie.

I'd like to think I haven't changed too much in that time. It's probably for others to judge that ultimately. But I can say with absolute certainty that Bob hasn't altered one tiny bit. He has remained the same, Zen-like cat through-out. He has travelled the world, met thousands of people, appeared on count-less TV shows. Yet he has remained chilled and content, from Berlin to Tokyo, Truro to Glasgow.

He has had his odd moment of grumpi-ness. Who doesn't? But in the main, he has barely uttered a growl of complaint. He simply sits there swishing his tail rhythmic-ally, sometimes purring quietly, putting a smile on people's faces as he does so, includ-ing mine. The joy it gives me to see him bringing such happiness to others is beyond words. The knowledge that he is happy and content in doing so makes it even more precious.

They say that a problem shared is a prob-lem halved. Well, I think the opposite is also true. Good fortune shared is good fortune doubled.

Faith in Friends Repays Itself

My stomach was churning as I led Bob in front of the lights and cameras that had been set up on an alleyway between Bow Street and Drury Lane.

It was a couple of weeks into the filming of *A Street Cat Named Bob* and the director Roger Spottiswoode was keen to experiment with Bob 'acting' in a scene. I had been unsure, but he and the producer Adam Rolston had persuaded me that this was a good opportunity.

The scene they had chosen involved Luke Treadaway, the actor playing me, sitting on the pavement, busking. It was a scene Bob knew inside out – he'd lived it for years.

But as I led him there I was racked with doubt. Would he be happy doing this?

Even if he was, would he be able to do what was required of him? I didn't want to let anyone down. And I certainly didn't want to waste the very expensive film crew's time.

The cameras had barely begun rolling when Bob did something amazing. As the stream of extras walked past, dropping and clinking coins into the guitar case, Bob began nodding at each of them, as if to say 'thanks'.

The crew's faces were a picture. You could see people asking themselves the same question: 'Did I just see what I just saw?' They had. And they saw it again on the next 'take', and the next one.

From then on, Bob appeared in as many scenes as was possible. He was working alongside a team of specialist ginger cats that had been brought over from Canada and trained to do the more difficult, action shots. Bob couldn't do those. They were left to his 'bobbelgangers'.

I learned a huge amount during those few, surreal weeks. But the lesson Bob taught me that night was perhaps one of the most important. Have faith. Believe in the friends who believe in you. If you do, they will repay that faith.

You Can't Lose a Real Friend

During the course of our years together, Bob has run away from me twice. Both incidents happened early on during our time together when Bob got scared, first by a street entertainer and then by a very aggressive dog.

We were reunited on each occasion, but it didn't mean the separations weren't hard. During the – thankfully brief – periods that

Bob and I were apart, I felt a nagging pain, as if there was something wrong with a part of me. It was only afterwards that I recognised what that meant.

The only friends you can lose are those who aren't really friends at all.

You can never lose a true friend. Even if you are separated. That friendship lives on inside you. It is a part of each of you. It doesn't go away.

PART TWO

It's a Bob's Life – What
We Need to Be Happy

We are all in search of fulfilment. But how and where do we find it? What are the foundation stones, the must-have ingredients for a contented existence? In other words, what do we need to be happy?

It's something I've often asked myself during my past decade with Bob. He has been instrumental in guiding me to some of the answers.

We All Need to Be Noticed

Once he and I had settled into our life together, Bob loved nothing more than being stroked or fussed over. I got the distinct impression that no one had spoiled him for a very long time, that he had been deprived of attention.

It pleased me that I was able to provide that attention, but it upset me, too. I kept imagining his previous life, kept seeing him sleeping in alleyways, being ignored by people. Getting no attention at all.

I didn't need to imagine what that felt like. I knew all too well from my time living on the streets. Like him I'd been ignored, marginalised; I'd disappeared, become an invisible man. And so I also understood that his happiness with me was a reaction to being made to feel important. Special.

We all need to be noticed. We all need to feel we are important. That we are needed.

We All Need a Routine

The routine into which we eventually settled was key in making Bob a calmer, more contented cat. He was less animated and agitated if he ate at the same time: first thing in the morning and early in the evening, around six. If he was then free to have a nap, he became even less erratic. Less on edge.

Later on too, as our relationship settled into a regular working pattern, that routine became even more entrenched. By then it was summertime and I would head into Covent Garden to busk later in the day.

The crowds were more numerous – and generous – in the late afternoon and evening.

It generally took us three quarters of an hour or so to get into the city, so in order to make the evening rush, we'd need to leave home before 5 p.m. Bob used to head to the door at 4.30 p.m. exactly. He'd finish off whatever food he had, then position himself there. It was as if he was saying: 'Hurry up, mate, we've got a bus to catch.'

I could have set my watch to him. In fact, on more than one occasion he had acted as an alarm, hurrying me up when my mind was elsewhere.

I now see that need for certainty is something universal – something that each and every one of us feels. Routine gives us parameters, but more importantly, it makes us feel secure.

We All Need Our Space

The more I got to know Bob – and his feline ways – the more I got to see that he and I were not so different after all. And once I realised that, I also began to understand what would make him feel at home.

For example, I had heard that territory is hugely important to cats. It's why they use the scent glands on their paws and in their claws to leave scent trails wherever they go. It is why they rub up and scratch furniture – and us, apparently. It provides them with assurance that their space is 'safe'.

Early on I had dissuaded Bob from doing it, gently pushing him away when he started scratching at the legs of a battered old chair in the corner.

It was when a friend visited me with his dog, a black Labrador, that the penny dropped. On first seeing the dog, Bob arched his back, made hissing noises and retreated to a safe corner. The dog barked back a couple of times, but soon settled. Bob watched him like a hawk. The minute the dog was out of the door, he leapt into action, striding around the flat, rubbing and scratching at everything.

'He's reclaiming his territory,' I said to myself.

We all like our space. We all prefer it to be a certain way and 'mark' it so that it is identifiably ours with our choice of furniture, colour schemes, paintings and photos on the wall. And we can get upset if other people invade that space and disrupt the balance.

Ever since then, I have let Bob get on with it. He rubs up against me, the furniture, door frames, radiators. Anything that makes him feel like his territory is established – and safe.

We All Need to Be Independent

Bob has always been self-sufficient. I think it stems from his days on the streets, looking after himself.

He seems to have learned that, if you need something in life, it is usually best to rely on yourself to provide it. The chances are that no one else will.

Early on, for instance, he learned to open cupboard doors so that he could look for food. He also learned to go to the toilet on his own, and once – to my amazement – used the toilet in my flat.

In recent years, he has got even more resourceful. In my new house, Bob can turn the handles on doors, especially the one leading into the kitchen, where I keep his food and water bowl on the floor.

Even more impressively, he has learned how to turn the tap on one of the sinks upstairs. He loves watching the running water and, when he's feeling a bit overheated, will dip his paw in and lick it to quench his thirst.

It always makes me smile. But it also reinforces something important. We all need to be independent. We all need to feel like we can control our lives.

We All Want to Feel Protected

We were out in central London one day, early on in our time together, when there was a loud explosion nearby. At first there was panic. We live in dangerous times. People didn't know what had happened, whether to hide or run for safety. After a while, however, it calmed down.

Bob had been walking alongside me. He had reacted to the bang instantly and had jumped up on to my shoulders. I'd been too wrapped up in the drama to really notice. But as things calmed down, I realised that he was still there – wrapped tightly around my neck.

He'd taken to riding on my shoulders when we were walking around central London, but this was the first time I'd seen him jump there as a reflex, as if seeking out a safe haven. I was touched. It underlined the feeling I had that he felt safe, protected in my company. And that safety was one of the reasons why he had decided to live with me.

We all need to feel that safety. That we are protected by someone or something.

We All Need to Be Ourselves

I had taken Bob into the park off the Embankment, near where we had been busking around Charing Cross station. I decided to sit down and take a break, while he did his business in the bushes.

He was attached to a long, string lead, which I could lengthen. After a while I felt a tugging on the line, as if I was a fisherman who had landed a fish. He was trying to get deeper into the bush. I stood up and fed him some more string. I assumed he wanted to find the right spot.

It was a couple of minutes later when he emerged. He did so with a small mouse in his teeth. It was alive and wriggling, desperately trying to escape. I was about to intervene, when the mouse managed to escape. Bob had placed it on the ground for a second and it had made a run for it. It scampered off at lightning speed.

I shouldn't have been surprised. Cats are predatory creatures. If we were going to be out in the world together, incidents like this were going to happen. It brought something home to me.

None of us are angels. We are all imperfect creatures. But we are who we are. It is in our nature. So many people try to change others – to mould them into something they are not. I wasn't going to do that.

Bob is a strong personality and I wanted him to be himself. Looking back on it, I think it was another of the reasons he stayed with me. None of us want to be prisoners of other people's ideas about who we should be. We all need to be free to be ourselves.

We All Need Something to Believe In

We were sitting on the pavement in the West End one evening, when a well-dressed guy emerged from the tube station concourse, walked to a spot a dozen or so metres from us and erected a placard.

It read: 'Believe in the Lord'.

I left him to it. My salvation depended on selling another dozen copies of *The Big Issue* before the evening rush hour ended.

The guy soon started preaching, reading from the Bible, but few people paid him any attention. Some were openly abusive to him.

I admired his resilience. He believed in something, I thought to myself.

For a moment I watched him, fascinated, a question forming in my mind.

Hmm, I thought. What do I believe in?

Just then Bob perked up and let out a meow. It was his 'I'm hungry' meow.

I reached into my rucksack and dug out a treat, then bent down to feed him. He leaned into my hand and rubbed his head against it, purring quietly.

I smiled to myself. I had my answer.

'You are what I believe in, Bob,' I said.

It was true. He had given me a new approach to life. A different perspective. He'd also given me purpose. Something to focus on, a shape to my day-to-day life. A structure that hadn't been there before.

In some sense, Bob must have felt the same way, too. He needed something to believe in as well, I guess. I think we all do.

We All Need Our Own Patch

It was a sunny weekend afternoon, a short time after Bob and I had moved into our new house, in the Surrey suburbs. I'd come downstairs to find Bob wasn't anywhere to be seen.

Instinctively I went out into the small garden where, in the past few days, he had begun to explore his new surroundings, sniffing the grass and the plants and watching the birds in the trees overhead. Sure enough, I glimpsed his distinctive ginger coat disappearing over the garden fence, backing on to some open ground beyond.

I was surprised. Bob wasn't a cat that wandered particularly. He liked to stay close to home. So whilst I was concerned, I didn't panic immediately.

After a couple of hours, however, I began to grow more nervous. Evening was closing in and I didn't want him to be out overnight. So I returned to the garden and started shouting for him. There was no sign of him.

I was just about to head back into the house when I heard noises. I recognised the sound instantly: it was two cats confronting each other.

I found Bob and a large, black cat a few feet apart on the fence alongside the house. The instant he saw me, Bob leapt off and literally jumped into my arms. It was as if we'd been separated for years – not a few hours.

It was obvious what had been going on. He had been doing what everyone needs to do to a greater or lesser extent when they move home, getting to know the lie of the land, marking out his own patch. Satisfied that he'd done that, he had run for home. He hasn't strayed from the garden since.

We All Need Things to Treasure

The sound of me doing the weekly hoovering in the living room had sent Bob scuttling off upstairs. He didn't much like it.

I'd not cleaned under the sofa for a while, so decided to slide it across the carpet to get the hoover underneath. I had been amazed at what I found.

It was like an Aladdin's cave of Bob's stuff.

He is regularly given and sent toys by fans from all over the world and plays with lots of them. Somehow, he had dragged a collection of toy animals, balls and assorted toys here. But this wasn't all. Bob had developed a habit of playing with plastic bottle lids that he found in the kitchen.

He had somehow hoarded about a dozen of them as well.

I threw the lids in the bin, but put the toys back into the large box in the hall.

I was intrigued. Why had he hoarded like this?

It wasn't too long after we had moved house. Had he been concerned that this new environment may contain other cats or animals who might steal his toys? Or was it his way of making sure his toys were safe from me? He had seen me bring in new furniture – and get rid of some other things. Was he concerned about me throwing his toys away?

Whatever the explanation, one thing was clear. These things were important to him. Knowing they were there made him feel safe and secure. Thinking about it, again, I realised that I was no different.

I was protective of certain things – photos, gifts from fans, books, mementoes from my travels – and had made sure I had safe places to keep them, in my living room and office. It was less to do with the fact they were worth anything, but more because they were of immense value to me.

It's all part of that need to feel that our home – and the precious things that make it feel like a home – are safe and secure.

We All Need Insecurity, Too

I had just moved into my new home and taken delivery of some flatpack furniture, which I'd slowly begun assembling. The hallway was filled with empty cardboard boxes, plastic bubble wrap and bits of polystyrene.

Bob, naturally, was fascinated by this. To him the chaotic pile of rubbish was an adventure playground, which he had to explore at every possible opportunity.

I had just finished putting together a coffee table in the living room when I noticed him playing there.

He was fixated by the bubble wrap and polystyrene. He was fascinated by the squeaking noises they made. He was also drawn to the boxes. One at a time, he climbed into the smaller ones, as if testing them to see which would make the best bed later. I didn't have the heart to tell him that it was all going into a recycling bin when I finished assembling everything.

The taller cardboard boxes that had contained the cabinets, were leaning up against each other, supporting each other like some sort of abstract art sculpture. Bob decided to climb it. The construction was very flimsy and I had a feeling he would be too heavy, but left him to it.

Sure enough, he'd just scaled the peak of the little cardboard mountain when *whoomph*, the whole edifice collapsed. Nimble and agile creature that he was, he jumped off, looking slightly miffed that his fun had been cut short.

I couldn't stop myself from laughing.

It struck me that we all need security, but sometimes we need insecurity, too. Some surprise elements that provide us with challenges and chances to learn. It helps us to grow. To learn. And if we can do so while having some fun as well, then all the better.

PART THREE

Being Bob – How to Get the Most Out of Life

Cats are experts at getting the most from life. They know what they want and know how to get it. And they execute their plans with laser-like efficiency. Bob is a master at squeezing the most from every day. He has strategies for success that would put even the most brilliant business minds to shame.

But he also seems to know how to enjoy and savour life, too. How to extract the positive from every situation. How to have the maximum fun. Spending time with him has opened my eyes to some of the secrets of his success. And it's made me wonder whether – at least, every now and again – we'd all benefit from being a little like Bob.

Think Slow, Act Fast

It is fascinating to watch the way Bob makes a decision. Before he does so, he will often sit there, like some little Buddha, slowly mulling over the choices in front of him. You can almost hear the machinations in his brain. Tick. Tick. Tick.

It doesn't matter what it is. He might be wondering whether to go for a stretch, a snooze or head to his bowl for something to eat. He will only take action when he's ready. Not a second earlier, not a second later.

When he makes his move, however, he is decisive. *Boom*. There's no hesitation. He knows what he wants and how to get it. And he generally does. He acts fast and gets results.

In a world where too many of us are indecisive or make snap decisions that we come to regret, we'd do well to take a leaf out of Bob's book.

To think slow, but act fast.

Believe in Yourself

Cats aren't weighed down by a lack of self-confidence. They don't harbour any self-doubt, at all. As far as we can tell, at least.

They seem to know what they want and are determined to get it.

I have a strong feeling that this is one of the keys to Bob's general wellbeing. He always exudes self-confidence. He seems totally comfortable in his own skin. We could all learn from it. We are all weighed down by insecurities and self-doubt.

I know it isn't easy, but we all have strengths and qualities that we can draw upon to give us confidence in ourselves. If we believe in ourselves, the world looks a very different place.

Our Happiness Lies Within

Bob can spend hours entertaining himself. He can fill half the day lying on the window-sill, watching the world go by. At our old flat in north London, he would watch the clouds floating by, the rain falling, the people and traffic passing by – anything and everything had the potential to entertain him. He's the same at our new home. He will lie there staring out into the garden, quietly mesmerised by the world outside.

Watching him, it often strikes me that he embodies something very simple, yet very profound. Something that a lot of people struggle to understand. There's a very famous Chinese saying: 'Happiness is the absence of the striving for happiness.'

What I think that means is that our happiness isn't dependent on others. It isn't something that we have to chase after. It actually lies within ourselves.

Bob seems to know that.

Open Your Eyes

During his days on the street, Bob loved nothing more than sitting with me on the pavement on a sunny day, quietly watching the world rushing past. He would take in everything. In his own laid-back way, of course.

Sometimes it would seem like his eyes were closed, but he missed nothing. It might be a bird scavenging for food in a nearby bin, a street performer setting up, a passer-by with an interesting outfit. He would quietly raise his head and zoom in. He would then watch or listen; fascinated, absorbing it all. It was as if he knew there was something to be gained from the experience. Something new, enlightening or simply entertaining to see.

We walk around with our eyes open, but there are times when we might as well have them closed. We are too busy, too wrapped up in our day-to-day lives to see what's in front of us.

We miss out on so much as a result.

There's Wonder All Around Us

Bob has an amazing effect on people. Men and women would often come across him lying on the pavement and be moved to tears. It was as if they'd discovered hidden treasure or a long lost relative. They would sit down and stroke him for a few minutes and be transformed. And often they weren't even cat lovers.

It made me wonder about the way we see the world. When people are looking for inspiration, they always tend to look upwards. To the skies. To the heavens. It's only natural. We are always being told that it's where the real wonder of life lies. Reach for the stars, we are told. Never reach for the gutter.

And yet, it seemed to me, at least, that by looking for inspiration in unexpected places, our imaginations, our minds – and best of all our hearts – might be opened up even more.

There is beauty and wonder there, too, if we only take the trouble to see it.

If You See a Chance, Take It

Like every other cat in the world, Bob is an opportunist. He will make the most of any opportunity that is presented to him.

It might be the offer of a snack or a treat. It might be an invitation to have his tummy tickled or go off for an exploratory walk in the bushes in the park. Whatever it is, his attitude is – if it's there, I am going to accept it.

In those situations, he doesn't humm and haah endlessly. He doesn't weigh up the pros and cons for very long. He sees the door – and then goes through it. There are times in all our lives, when we would do well to take the same approach.

If you see a chance, take it.

Don't Dwell on the Small Stuff

There's a well known book called 'Don't Sweat the Small Stuff'. Its basic message is simple: don't fixate on the tiny irritations or setbacks in life. Let them go. Put them into the proper perspective. Don't turn them into big stuff that makes you stressed and unhappy.

Bob seems to instinctively operate according to that philosophy.

It's rare that he gets into a confrontation with another cat or a dog, for instance, but even if he does, he doesn't seem to let it get under his skin. Once that confrontation has run its course, he will almost always walk away. Regardless of the outcome.

We humans don't do this easily. We are prone to seek revenge or retribution. To stew on even the smallest things, take them personally. I can't know exactly what goes on in Bob's brain, but he seems to simply gets on with it. It's as if he knows that feeling angry or vengeful is a waste of time. I have a strong suspicion that it's one of the reasons he lives such a seemingly contented existence.

Be Appreciative

Like all cats, Bob seems to live in the present. Who knows whether he thinks about the past, or the future? What's quite clear is that in his day-to-day life, he deals in the here and now.

If he wants to grab a snooze, it doesn't matter if it is on a cold pavement or on a comfortable sofa. It makes no difference to him. He will curl himself up and nod off, oblivious to whatever is going on around him.

It's the same at meal times. It doesn't matter if his food bowl contains a few handfuls of biscuit or a feast of gourmet tuna, he will gobble it down just the same. His attitude is: that's my meal. I'll eat what's in front of me.

I've often watched him and wondered whether there's a lesson there for all of us. The fact is that none of us is ever going to get everything that we want in life. None of us. We can work and strive to make things better, but we will never get all we want. It's impossible.

And that means that, as we go through life, we have a choice.

We can either get wrapped up in that: be obsessed with what we don't have, and the fact that we won't ever have it. Or we can appreciate what we do have.

Seize Each Day

I watch Bob some mornings and envy him. He wakes himself up, tucks into his breakfast and heads into his new day unencumbered by what happened yesterday or the day before.

To him, each morning marks the beginning of not only a new day, but a new opportunity to be content and happy. A chance to enjoy all that life has to offer him.

I often tell myself that it's not a bad philosophy to adopt. Especially when life seems hard. If you can forget about what happened yesterday and treat today as a fresh start, you are already halfway towards ensuring that today is a better one.

Know Your Limitations

For all his confidence, it is rare that Bob bites off more than he can chew. It's as if he knows his limitations. He is aware not to be too ambitious.

It's almost as though he knows that old Chinese saying: 'A bird can roost but on one branch and a mouse can drink no more than its fill from a river.'

It is something I tell myself often.

We should all know – and accept – our limitations.

There's Something Good
in Every Day

Life on the streets could be miserable. I was
ignored, abused – even spat at, on
occasion.

But Bob was always there to cheer me
up. It might be a silly thing he did, or simply
a moment with him on the bus when he
curled up next to me. Whenever he did that,
I was reminded of something universal.

While, every day may not be good, there's
something good in every day.

Let the Sun Shine In

Bob and I spent much of our first summer
together sitting on the pavement near
Covent Garden, busking in the rush hour. It

wasn't the greatest of summers, weather-wise. The days were often overcast, the sun was an infrequent visitor.

Whenever it did appear in the skies, however, I noticed that it had an instant effect on Bob. He would spend most of his days curled up in a ball, quietly watching the flow of tourists and shoppers rushing past us.

The moment the sun arrived in the sky above us, though, he was a cat on a mission. He would begin shifting himself around, moving in and out of the shadows as he worked out the sunniest spot. He would then stretch his body out on the floor, elongating himself so as to get the maximum benefit.

Often it would be a fleeting opportunity. The sun would quickly disappear behind a new, passing cloud. But it didn't bother Bob one bit. He was always determined to make the absolute most of every ray of sunshine that was available.

It always made me smile to myself. I was full of admiration for him – and his philosophy. Life is short. Sometimes you have to squeeze every ounce of joy and pleasure you can from it. The sun doesn't always shine. If it's there, you should let it in.

Pick Your Battles

It was a bright summer's day and Bob was facing a dilemma. On the one hand, he was very happy lying on the sill of the open window as the sun streamed into our living room. On the other he was irritated by the bees that had been attracted to the flowers at the top of the garden near the window. He wanted them to buzz off.

For a few moments, I watched him weighing up his options. He was clearly asking himself: 'Can I get them?'

If it had been inside the house, it would have been a different story. But it was clear it would take a precision strike to leap through the window out on to the flower bed and to catch the bees. It was almost impossible, a million to one shot, but he kept mulling it over. Along with something else.

The other thing that was annoying him was a box of tissues on the sill. He'd parked himself tight up against it and was clearly unhappy that it was there. The sun was shining at its brightest in that exact spot.

It took him a minute or so to complete his calculations. As he did so, he looked back and forth between the bees outside and the box of tissue next to him. What to do?

When he made his move, it was decisive. In a smooth movement, he swished at the tissue box with his paw, flipping it off the sill on to the floor so that he now had the best spot. He then proceeded to splay himself out on the sill, soaking up the sunshine. The bees were forgotten.

It was an object lesson. If you are faced with a problem that you can do something about – then do something. But if you can't do anything – let it go.

Focus on what you can change. Forget about what you cannot. Life will be much simpler and enjoyable if you do.

Curiosity Doesn't Kill the Cat

If there's one expression that leaves me scratching my head, it is this: curiosity killed the cat.

I really don't get it. Curiosity, to my mind, is an intrinsic part of a cat's make-up. It is actually a life-saver, something that adds to their day-to-day existence.

Bob certainly loves exploring. Wherever we go, he will scout out his surroundings. He won't sit down contentedly until he's checked out the location fully. He will spend ages sniffing and shoving his head into nooks and crannies, rooting around until he is satisfied he has seen all there is to see.

It's partly an instinctive cat trait. He wants to feel safe and secure. He is marking out his territory. But it's partly, too, because he's curious – and, to judge from the way he wags his tail and nonchalantly strolls around, exploring the world around him makes him happy.

Too many of us lead incurious lives. Too many of us are afraid to try something new. Too many want to stick to the well-worn path, rather than following the uncharted one where we can leave our own trail. We should all embrace the unknown sometimes.

Curiosity doesn't kill anyone or anything. Quite the opposite – it is the source of some of the best things in life.

Always Enjoy the Journey

We were out walking in a nearby park one windy, autumn day, when Bob spotted a small pile of fallen leaves. They had been blown by the wind and had formed into a small pyramid. Bob jogged over to it, then waded into the pile until he was so deep into the leaves I could barely see his legs. He then began thrashing away, frantically clearing leaves away with his paws.

It was hilarious. For a while he was lost in a flurry of brown, gold and silver leaves.

It was impossible for me to know what was going through his mind. Perhaps he had decided there was something hidden under the leaves? Maybe he smelled a mouse or some food?

It wasn't long before the pyramid had been flattened, reduced to a blanket of leaves. Sure enough, there was something lying on the grass now, glinting in the afternoon sun. Unfortunately, it wasn't as exciting as Bob might have hoped. It was a battered, old Coke can.

He nudged it with his nose, to check it was as unpromising as it appeared. He then jogged away, eager to explore another, smaller pile of leaves, the disappointment of the previous one already forgotten.

Sitting on a bench nearby, watching the scene unfold, I couldn't help smiling. I was reminded me of that old saying: 'To travel hopefully is a better thing than to arrive'. We place so much emphasis on achieving our goals, on reaching our destinations, that we often forget to enjoy the journey.

We should follow Bob's example and simply relish the journey for what it is, regardless of where it takes us.

Take Things Little by Little

I was working in my living room one morning, when I heard a noise in the kitchen.

I found Bob standing at the foot of the fridge looking up, fixated on something.

One of his favourite treat sticks was balancing precariously on the edge of the fridge. I must have left it there.

It wasn't long before his teatime, and I didn't want him snacking now. So I ignored it and went back to work. I was writing a reply to an email that had made me a little angry. I wanted to vent my frustration.

Out of the corner of my eye, I saw him pacing around. He then jumped up on to the worktop near the fridge, about five feet away from the treat.

He had a dilemma. If he jumped up at it and nudged the fridge, he risked knocking the treat down the side where he would never be able to get to it. He was sitting there studying the situation. Weighing up his options.

I looked away, returning to my email.

A moment or two later, I looked again. Bob had now nudged a packet of biscuits into position beneath the treat and was standing on it, stretching upwards. With the most delicate movement of his paw, he nudged the treat in the right direction. He then got down, repositioned himself and did it again. He did that three times, but then on the fourth, the treat tipped off the edge and fell . . . on to the kitchen floor.

Mission accomplished.

I'd written a rather harsh email, but hadn't yet hit 'send'. As I fed Bob the contents of the treat, I decided against it. I did so later, but in more temperate language. And I got the result I wanted in the process.

Sometimes you have to achieve your goals by stealth. Intelligently. Patiently.

Little by little.

PART FOUR

Bob vs the World – How to Survive All That Life Throws at Us

It is often said that knowledge comes from learning, while wisdom comes from living. It has always struck me as being very true. So much of our so-called knowledge comes to us second-hand, from books, through film or television. Very few of us know things through first-hand experience.

I am frequently reminded of this when I look at Bob. He has not learned about life second-hand. All the wisdom he has acquired has come to him the hard way, from the years he spent on the streets, coping with people and situations of all kinds.

It is why I have always found it so interesting to try to understand that wisdom. And why it is so valuable. He has taught me a lot about coping with – and maybe even learning from – everything life has to throw at us.

Don't Let a Bad Yesterday
Spoil a Good Today

Bob's ability to shake off bad experiences was summed up by an experience we had one evening in central London. We had been heading home after a busy day doing interviews and promoting the movie, *A Street Cat Named Bob.*

I was about to hail a cab, when someone started shouting at me. It was a fairly well-to-do lady, probably in her sixties. She was in an animated state, waving a stick at me.

'That's cruelty to animals,' she shouted. 'You shouldn't have him on a lead. I'm going to report you to the RSPCA.'

I stopped and tried to talk to her. But she wasn't having any of it.

Bob had sensed that she wasn't a kind soul and had positioned himself defensively on my shoulder. I knew from experience that if this lady made a move, Bob would lash out at her. I really didn't want that to happen. That wasn't the kind of publicity we wanted! Fortunately, a black cab appeared with its yellow lights on. I hailed it and jumped in.

On the drive home, it ate away at me. I'd worked so hard all day. I'd spoken to journalists and TV presenters for hours, constantly promoting the positive, hopeful message of our story. The exchange with the lady in the street had lasted for less than a minute, but it had somehow spoiled the previous eight or nine hours.

But then I looked at Bob, lying on the leather seat of the cab, licking himself and gently purring away. He looked completely content. The confrontation with the woman had set him on edge as well. But he had brushed it off. It had been forgotten.

'You're right,' I said to him. 'What's the old expression: you shouldn't let a good today be ruined by a bad yesterday.'

Wisdom Is the Daughter of Experience

Since his earliest days with me, Bob has always seemed at his most focused when he feels under threat. His eyes dart around, his ears prick up and his tail points upwards. It's as if he is primed for anything – and prepared for the worst.

This is natural, animal instinct, of course, but I've often wondered whether it is also to do with his background, the hardships he suffered during his early days on the streets. Was he once attacked by a dog, for instance?

Is that why he is wary of some aggressive breeds?

Regardless of the past, the key thing is that he has learned from that experience. Wisdom, in his case, is very much the daughter of experience. The wisest of us are those that, like Bob, draw the biggest lessons from the hardship life throws at us.

Don't Be Ruled by Fear

Like all of us, Bob has a few dislikes and quirks. A few things that make him bristle or grow restless. He loathes the sound that lorries with hydraulic brakes make, for example. He can also get agitated by aggressive dogs and people. He doesn't like really loud music too much either, especially now he's getting older.

In general, however, he allows little to frighten or upset him. He relies on his experience. He simply keeps his eyes and ears – and his highly sensitive whiskers – open. And if he is unsure of something or someone, he reacts immediately. He will fight, freeze or take flight. He will deal with the situation decisively.

We seem to live in a world that is now filled with anxieties. People are crippled by fears, some genuine, but some completely irrational. We could all learn a lesson from Bob. He is careful and keeps his eyes open. But he doesn't let fear rule his world.

Don't Judge a Book by its Cover

Spending his days and nights on the streets, Bob saw human nature at its best and worst. Most of those he came across were kind to him, but some were mean. It gave him a very strong instinct about people.

Now if he senses a good, warm-hearted person, he calmly lets them approach and stroke him. But Bob can sniff or spot someone who is out to hurt or harm him from a mile away. And if he feels a threat, he soon lets them know. His hiss is quite something to behold. He has protected me from potential threats on more than one occasion.

What's important is that his judgment has nothing to do with appearances. How someone looks, the way they dress, or the colour of their skin. It's about what's going on inside, whether they are a good person or a bad one.

He never judges a book by its cover.

Guard Against Unguarded Thoughts

I always try to follow Bob's example. I do my best to judge people not by their appearance, but by the person I sense is inside.

It doesn't always work.

One morning during the filming of the movie in Covent Garden, I spotted a guy hovering a short distance away from where Bob and I were waiting to be called in front of the cameras.

He was a tall, lean figure in a scruffy denim jacket, jeans and trainers. He seemed on edge. I was wary immediately. There was a lot of expensive equipment around. Who knew what his intentions were? Was he planning on stealing something? Or worse, harming Bob?

I moved towards him.

'Whatever idea you might have, mate, forget it,' I said.

He looked confused.

'No, James. I'm not here to cause trouble. I'm Simon.'

Now it was my turn to be confused.

'Simon? Simon who? And how do you know my name?' He smiled.

'Simon from Centre Point. Five years ago. We shared a room. Don't you remember?'

I just froze.

'Oh my God.'

The two of us embraced like the long-lost friends we were.

Years earlier, we'd both been homeless and had taken refuge at the same charity centre. We'd drifted apart. Simon now lived in Glasgow, but had heard of Bob and me and come to see us. He'd been keeping a respectful distance, waiting for filming to end before coming to say hello.

It was a sobering reminder. When I was on the streets, people had always jumped to the wrong conclusions about me. Just because I was busking, it didn't mean I was a bad person. Now I'd been guilty of the same thing. I'd failed to abide by Bob's lesson and judged a book by its cover.

There's another old saying: 'Your worst enemy cannot harm you as much as your own unguarded thoughts.' This encounter taught me to be on guard more often.

Keep Facing the Sun

The abuse I received working on the streets was a constant part of my life. Almost every day someone would shout something behind my back. You never get used to it, but you do learn to live with it.

There were times when I would bite, and engage the person abusing me. It was a pointless exercise, however. There was no benefit in interacting with people, who – in all honesty – didn't deserve any interaction in the first place. I only upset myself by doing so.

Having Bob with me helped enormously. He almost physically forced me to take a different approach. He would sit on my shoulders, his face pointing forward, looking ahead rather than back. It struck me one sunny, summer's evening, while we were walking through Covent Garden, heading towards Leicester Square where I was due to meet a friend. Some idiot had just shouted abuse at me, but I ignored it. I pressed on with Bob on my shoulder, heading towards the sun, setting to the west.

'What's the old saying, Bob?' I said quietly to him. 'Keep your face always towards the sunshine – and the shadows will fall behind you.'

Sometimes Not Getting What You Want Is Good for You

There's an old Buddhist saying: 'Sometimes not getting what you want is a wonderful stroke of luck.' I hadn't really understood its full meaning until early on during my time with Bob, when my life took a dramatic turn.

Bob and I had been struggling to make ends meet busking around Covent Garden. I'd regularly run into trouble with the authorities and had a particularly bad relationship with the staff at the Covent Garden tube station, who objected to me and Bob sitting outside. Matters had come to a head when I'd been falsely accused of abusing a ticket inspector. I had been arrested and stuck in a prison cell overnight.

I'd been cleared of the charge eventually, but it had given me a wake-up call. I'd dreamed of using my busking as a launching pad for a musical career. But a night in a cold cell had made me realise – in the short term, at least – I simply wasn't going to be able to achieve that. I had Bob to care for, as well as myself. I had to make a change.

As it turned out, it was the best thing that could have happened to me. Instead I started selling *The Big Issue*, initially in the West End, but then at the Angel in Islington. It was there that my life was transformed. I was spotted by a literary agent and asked to write a book about my life with Bob.

I often think back to that turning point. I had been fortunate in so many ways. First, I'd been able to escape an unjust accusation, but more importantly, I'd been forced to make a change.

Of course, I could never have predicted the precise direction my life was going to take from that point. But there was no doubt that in not getting what I'd wanted, I really had enjoyed the most miraculous good luck.

Wherever You Lay Your Hat

During the making of the movie, Bob and I had to spend a lot of time at Twickenham Film Studios.

It was a very alien environment. The lights, the noise and the unfamiliar faces would have put ninety-nine per cent of cats into a spin, I'm fairly certain. But, despite a little jitteriness at first, Bob adapted quickly.

He would nap when he felt like it. Head off exploring when he wanted.

He worked hard, too. The set designers had created a replica of my flat in north London, where Bob and Luke Treadaway spent their days performing to the cameras. It was long, hard work, but he didn't mind.

The instant Bob heard the tell-tale sound of the bell and saw the recording light in the studio turn from red to green, signalling that filming was over, he would follow the power lines out of the door and up to his dressing room, where he would expect to be fed. There was never a shortage of volunteers. Half the crew carried packets of Dairylea Dunkers or Dreamies with them, ready to cater to Bob's every whim.

Towards the end of filming, someone asked me why he'd adapted so well? It was a good question. My presence was, obviously, important. He felt safe in the knowledge his 'protector' was there. But it was more than that. Bob also liked routine. The predictability and orderliness of his daily existence on the film set made him feel at ease.

But most importantly, I think, Bob had learned that in life you sometimes have to put your head down wherever there's a warm bed. Life is about adapting. About making the most of what's in front of you. And sometimes that means making yourself

at home, regardless of where you may lay
your hat.

Expect Nothing

One evening, while Bob and I were busking
around Covent Garden, we were approached
by a very glamorous and attractive young
woman. To judge from the way she was
dressed – in a glittery black outfit with
dazzling jewellery around her neck that
must have been worth a small fortune – I

think she must have been on her way to the theatre or the opera in the nearby West End.

She saw Bob and me and stopped for a second.

'Oh, how sweet. What a beautiful cat,' she said, smiling, then taking a photograph on her rather expensive-looking phone.

It hadn't been the most profitable evening, so as I often did, I very politely suggested she pop a pound or two into my guitar case for the photo opportunity.

'Any contribution appreciated. It'll go towards a coffee or a treat for Bob here,' I said.

I might as well have asked her if I could pawn the necklace around her neck. Her face was transformed. The smile disappeared to be replaced by a scowl.

'How very impertinent of you,' she said, marching off in a huff.

Such encounters weren't unique. They

simply confirmed something that I'd come to understand even before Bob and I had got together. A truth that unfortunately applies, not only on the streets of London, but everywhere.

Often in life it is best to expect nothing, because that way you will never be disappointed.

Stand Your Ground

The streets of London aren't paved with gold. Quite the opposite. They can be intimidating and unsettling. And Bob had his fair share of scares.

During our days busking and selling *The Big Issue*, he was always particularly aware of dogs. Not necessarily because he was scared of them, but because he knew he had to handle them carefully.

His instincts were so strong that he could tell if a dog was an empty threat. All bark and no bite. A bully, in effect.

It happened very rarely, but in those instances, he would confront them. He would hiss or snarl or even slash his paws at them. It always worked. The dogs themselves either froze, or they fled. I saw Bob reduce several seemingly scary dogs to gibbering jelly.

And whenever he did so, I was reminded that the best way to deal with a bully is to call their bluff.

Judge Others by Actions Not Words

They say that the best way to judge a person's character is by their deeds rather than their words.

With cats, you have no option. You can *only* judge them on their deeds.

Bob has his mischievous moments, of course. And he can be difficult at times. But for more than a decade – through his daily deeds – Bob has displayed exactly the same character. He has been as warm, fun, loyal and caring a companion as anyone could wish to have. No words could convince me that he is otherwise.

Of all the things that Bob has taught me, it is one of the most valuable lessons.

I always try to judge others by the same standards. By their actions and not their words.

Don't Let Your Boat Take in Water

Bob's ability to shut out the rest of the world never ceases to amaze me. He seems to have the capacity to cope with almost any situation.

Perhaps the most unbelievable example of this came in November 2016, when he and I attended the royal premiere of the film of *A Street Cat Named Bob* in London.

It was one of the most surreal evenings of my life, something that, to this day, I can't quite believe happened to me. Bob and I had to appear on the red carpet, doing interviews and posing for photographs. There were dozens, perhaps hundreds of people there, from fans who had travelled to see the event, to television crews and banks of photographers flashing away with their cameras.

It was organised bedlam. At times it was hard to hear above the shouts of the fans, photographers and interviewers who wanted to stick a camera and a microphone in my face. Yet Bob – positioned throughout on my shoulder – sailed through it unfazed.

We spent what must have been half an hour on the red carpet and throughout that time he remained a picture of calm and composure. To be honest, I think he enjoyed it.

That night, everyone asked the same thing: 'How on earth does he do it?'

I can never know for sure, but I think he insulates himself from what is going on around him. I think he simply approaches life with the view that if it isn't directly affecting me, then I have nothing to fear from it.

Boats don't sink because of the water that's around them. Boats sink because of the water that gets into them.

Bob seems to have the gift of not allowing what happens around him to get inside him. He merely sails serenely on.

PART FIVE

The Zen of Bob – How to
Be Good to Ourselves

Cats know instinctively how to look after themselves. They don't need to go on fad diets, or hire personal trainers or masseurs to keep themselves fit. They don't need psychologists or life coaches to teach them how to live well.

They just know how to do it – while remaining chilled-out in the process.

That's certainly the case with Bob. Someone once described him as having an inner peace, a 'Zen-like calm' in everything he does. Watching him over the years, I've seen that we could all learn a little from his methods, and benefit from what you might call the Zen of Bob.

Bobfulness

Bob can spend an age staring at a tree full of birds. It's as if he is in a trance. He will sit there, absolutely still, his body coiled, his eyes darting around, picking up every tweet, every flap of a wing. I often wonder what fascinates him so much.

Is it something in his DNA, a hunting instinct? Does he want to get up there and attack them? Is it his fascination with their song? Or is he counting them?

I was watching a programme on TV one day about 'mindfulness' and how it helps the brain to focus on one thing for a few minutes. To think about it, look at it in detail. To get lost in that one small thing, to the exclusion of everything else that's going on around you.

It triggered a thought. That's what Bob is doing when he watches those birds, I smiled to myself.

He's practising Bobfulness.

Rich Cat, Poor Cat

In some ways, Bob's Zen-like calm is a reflection of the simplicity of his life. He has no bills to pay. No mortgage to fret over. No responsibilities.

Bob has no possessions at all. And in that he might be lucky.

It sometimes occurs to me that the more you have, the more you worry about losing it all.

Listen to Your Body

Bob always takes time to stretch. It's as if he's doing yoga or pilates or some other form of exercise. He seems to know instinctively which limbs, which muscles to exercise. It's as if his body has told him what is required.

It never ceases to impress me. And it makes me understand that our bodies are talking to all of us. All the time. Our problem is that most of the time we simply don't listen.

Make a Meal of Your Food

I sometimes watch Bob eating his food. It is fascinating to see. Sometimes he will start off eating eagerly, gobbling down a few mouthfuls. At other times he will inspect it carefully, sniffing and staring at it, as if checking its quality.

When he takes a mouthful, he makes the absolute most of it. He chews away for minutes sometimes, especially if it's a meaty treat that he particularly enjoys. It's as though nothing else matters at that precise moment. As if this is the most important thing in the world. It is a lesson for us.

Doctors, dieticians and wellness experts say that we need to relish and enjoy our food more. There are, apparently, massive benefits to slowing down and relishing every mouthful of food, every sip of a drink. That's because, by paying proper attention to the flavours, smells and textures of what we put in our mouths, even concentrating on the mechanics of eating, it can make us more aware of the sensations that make us feel alive. It can soothe our bodies, lift anxieties and stresses.

Maybe Bob knows this already. Perhaps that is why he puts such importance into eating his food.

S-L-O-W-L-Y Does It

Bob lives his life at his own speed. And that speed is usually pretty leisurely. He can hit the accelerator pedal sometimes. But in general, he will take things s-l-o-w-l-y.

We humans imagine we have too much to do and too little time in which to do it. We never allow ourselves an hour to do something that we can cram into ten or twenty minutes. We somehow think it's wasting time.

But the truth is the absolute opposite. The only thing being wasted is the experience. Especially if you'd benefit from taking an hour to do it. You are actually punishing yourself.

Why would you do that? Why wouldn't you also take things s-l-o-w-l-y?

Know Yourself

The way that Bob manages himself never fails to impress me. He understands himself perfectly, it seems.

He reminds me of one of the wisest pieces of Zen philosophy: 'Knowing others is intelligence; knowing yourself is true wisdom.'

Express How You Feel

Bob wastes no time in letting me know when he's feeling unwell. He makes no pretence about it. He will refuse to move or will lie on my bed, immobile. He will make mewling noises. It's all designed to get the message across: 'I'm not well.'

It is human instinct to deny pain. To soldier on. To deny that we've been hurt or are in discomfort. We leave it until it becomes unbearable.

It's a mistake, of course. Ignore an illness and it is likely to get twice as bad. By acting soon, you give yourself the best chance of recovery.

Tune in to Nature

Cats are tuned into nature in a way that we probably don't yet fully understand. They seem able to detect changes in the weather, and their eating and sleeping habits change considerably through the seasons.

Come the wintertime, for instance, Bob will sleep for hours on end. As the nights close in and the darkness descends, so he curls up and shuts out the outside world. He knows it's the season to hibernate, to recharge the batteries in readiness for spring.

When spring arrives, he sleeps less and is generally more active. Even his body adapts to the change, as he moults and then re-grows his coat according to the seasons.

We might all benefit from paying a little more attention to the natural cycle of things.

Say What You Mean, and Mean What You Say

Bob communicates using a mixture of sounds – from gentle purrs and growls, to hisses and blood-curdling screams. But he can also get his message across using body language, swishing and wagging his tail, or arching his body to make a particular point. What's most impressive about it all is its simplicity. If he's got something to say, he gets it across quickly and directly. There is never any room for doubt.

First thing in the morning, he will slide up along the bed and alert me to the fact that it's his breakfast time. He may use a variety of methods for this: from purring quietly to jumping forcefully on to my chest, or placing his face inches from mine and letting out an ear-piercing *meow*.

Whatever method he uses, however, his message is unmistakeable. I open my eyes and there he is, staring at me with an expression that says: 'Come on, get up, I'm hungry.'

I don't always appreciate it, especially if he wakes me at the crack of dawn on a cold, winter's morning. But in a world where we can all sometimes take a hundred words when one will do, I have come to admire his directness.

Bob doesn't do small talk. It's all big talk. He says what he means – and means what he says.

No Means No

With Bob, no means precisely that. No.

If he doesn't want to do something, then that's that. He won't do it. No treat, no enticement, no stroke of the head or back will move him. He has made up his mind. End of story. I might as well give up.

It actually makes life simpler. It keeps things black and white. There are no shades of grey. You accept his decision, and move on. You find an alternative route, or a different way of doing things. No matter how inconvenient or annoying it may be.

Sometimes, as adults, we all need to learn to say no. It's our right to do so. Clearly and simply and unambiguously. It may not make everyone happy, all the time. But at least people will know where you – and they – stand.

A Simple Thank You

Bob's tail is a signalling system all of its own.

If he is swishing it sharply from side to side, it means he is agitated or upset. But if it is moving more slowly and rhythmically – like a windscreen wiper – it's a sign of contentment. All is well in his world.

I've often wondered why he feels the need to signal this way. I'm sure it isn't for my benefit. Regardless, I always appreciate seeing that tell-tale, slow-motion wag. To me, it's as good as him writing me a thank-you note, or sending flowers or a box of chocolates.

If only others did the same, even unconsciously.

Silence Is Golden

Bob has a language all of his own – a highly effective system for communicating precisely what he wants to say. I find it fascinating to behold. It has taught me a lot of useful things about the art of communication.

There are days, for example, when Bob will sit alongside me barely making a sound from dawn 'til dusk. I never worry about it. It must mean that he is content. If he wasn't, he would let me know soon enough.

I often nod and smile wistfully at him. If only that were true in the human world, I think to myself. So many people speak when they have nothing to say. When they would also be better off appreciating that sometimes silence really is golden.

That the quieter you become, the more you can hear.

A Social Network

When Bob and I did our first book signings, I received a number of surprises. For a start, I was amazed – and genuinely moved – by the number of people who turned up to meet us. It was something of a miracle, as far as I was concerned. I didn't think anyone would be interested.

But the other really surprising thing was the way Bob reacted to all this attention. He seemed genuinely to lap it up. He didn't mind people stroking him, within reason. He remained completely in control. If he felt like napping, that's exactly what he did. And if it was time to go home, then he let me know that in no uncertain terms. But in the main he was happy to interact with people, especially those that had treats for him.

It set me thinking. There are lots of scientific studies that argue human health and wellbeing is improved by regular, social interaction. In short, isolation is bad for you, but mixing with people – even if it's for a chat in a shop or the park – is good for you.

I suspect, again, that cats know this. It's one of the reasons they have gravitated towards us humans.

Let the Love In

I'm sure everyone who has ever had or known a cat will agree with me on this universal truth: they never, ever refuse affection. Bob certainly doesn't. Start tickling him under his neck, or stroking the back of his neck, and he will press his head against you and lie there. It's as if he's saying: 'Yes, I deserve this attention, please continue.'

Sometimes, if he feels the need, he will flip himself over and spread himself out, inviting you to direct your tickling to his tummy instead. He absolutely loves it and can't get enough of it. I've never spent more than a few minutes stroking him, but I reckon if I carried on for an hour, he'd be perfectly happy.

It occurred to me once that we could all learn from this. Too many of us reject genuine and sincere affection, whether it is from a friend or a relative, or someone we love. I know I've been guilty of this. We do so for many reasons: fear, embarrassment, self-doubt.

It makes no sense when you think about it. Love is in short supply in this world, so when it is offered to us, we should all embrace it. We should all follow Bob's lead. We should all let the love in.

Have Fun – and Often

Bob is no different to other cats when it comes to play. He loves nothing more than to flip a favourite toy around the room, or to leap manically up and down trying to catch the sunbeams that are dancing on the wall. At Christmas, he can entertain himself for ages with a piece of used wrapping paper.

It's as though he is lost in his own world, motivated by who knows what. Is he trying to catch the mouse, or simply exhilarated by the fun of tossing it around the room? Is he intent on tearing the Christmas wrapping into pieces, or does he just love the sound and sensation of the crumpled paper? Who knows. And more importantly, who cares?

What's clear is that it provides him with entertainment, a break from his normal routine. And when he's doing it, the rest of the world is shut out completely. We all need to do that every now and again, don't we?

Don't Be Slaves to the Clock

Bob, like all cats, obeys his body clock. He knows when the day begins, and when it ends. When it's time to sleep and eat. *Especially*, when it's time to eat. But beyond that, time – as we know it – is of little importance to him. There is no clock dictating how he whiles away the hours each day.

We are very different, of course. We are slaves to the clock. We dwell on the passing of time, mourn the way moments flash by. We are constantly counting the hours, days, months and years.

We could learn a lot from Bob's attitude. We might live more enjoyable, more fulfilling lives. Maybe even longer ones, too?

Pay No Heed to What Others Think of You

Cats aren't burdened by worrying about what other cats think of them. Well, as far as we know, at least.

I'm pretty convinced that Bob isn't obsessed with his reputation. He's not concerned about how many people 'like' him on social media. (Even though many thousands do.) He isn't at all concerned with what people say about him publicly. He's oblivious to it. Bob just gets on with being himself. Living his day-to-day life and, in doing so, displaying his true character. If that appeals to people, then great. If it doesn't, no matter. He is who he is – and that's the way it is.

If only we could all adopt that attitude.

Too many of us are eaten up by worrying about what others think and say about us. We would be better off focusing on our true character rather than 'reputations' that can rise and fall for no good reason. Being ourselves, saying what we really feel.

That, after all, is the truth. And that's what counts in the end.

Live the Years, Don't Count Them

As I write, Bob is now around eleven years old. Perhaps older. As a housebound cat, there's every possibility he will live well into his teens, even into his twenties. He has no awareness of this, of course. He may be in his middle years now, but he is not going to have a mid-life crisis.

He isn't going to suddenly do something dramatic like buy a sports car or run off to a Buddhist retreat in Nepal. He's not going to totally re-invent himself because he is suddenly aware of his mortality.

We can never know this, but I imagine that ageing is simply something he feels. He is not counting the years. He is simply living them. Wouldn't we all benefit from thinking that way sometimes? None of us has to be defined by our chronological age.

Age really is just a number.

Don't Grow Up

Bob may be older, but he is definitely still in touch with his inner kitten. The younger, more playful part of him is always there.

Sometimes he will play with a toy, chase the reflection of glass on the wall. At other times he will find a cardboard box or a piece of paper and entertain himself by playing with it.

It's proof of something that I heard once: it is easier to grow old if you haven't entirely grown up. Perhaps we should all see the world that way.

It's the Life in Your Years

Even as he gets older, Bob lives his life to the full, doing precisely what he wants, when he wants to do it.

If he wants to spend his day curled up in a ball watching the world go by, he will do so. If he wants to spend it playing or chasing things around the house, he will do so. He is living on his own terms, oblivious to the passing of time.

Sometimes I look at him and think he is an embodiment of another old saying: 'It's not the years in your life that count, it's the life in your years.'

Stay Open to Change

As Bob has grown older, he has subtly changed his ways.

He gives himself more time to rest and recuperate. If he's had a busy day, he will sleep an extra hour. He may also start his day a little later the following morning. And he will not be rushed in that process. His eating habits have changed slightly, too. He prefers to eat soft food in the evening now – and likes to eat at 7.30 p.m. Precisely.

It has all happened naturally and seamlessly. It's as if his body is telling him that it needs to modify itself. It is something we could all learn from. We all need to stay open to change.

PART SIX

The University of Bob – Lessons in Day-to-Day Life

Sharing my life with Bob is an endless education. There's something new to be learned every day. Sometimes it is simply from watching him interacting with the world around him. At other times it's the situations that we find ourselves in – both at home and on our travels together.

It's as if I've enrolled as a lifetime student at the University of Bob.

Fall Down Seven Times, Get Up Eight

I'd arranged to get together with an old friend, Steve, for a drink one summer's evening.

We were in the middle of a heatwave, so we sat out in the beer garden. I hung my rucksack on a hook that was attached to the wall, about five feet off the ground. Bob sat on the bench beside me, lapping up the last rays of sunshine.

I left him and Steve while I popped inside to the bar. When I came back, Steve was smiling broadly.

'What's so funny?' I asked.

'Bob's been entertaining me,' he said.

'What's he been up to?'

'He's been trying to snatch something from your bag. I wasn't sure whether to let him have it or not,' he replied, pointing at the rucksack, and the distinctive colouring of a packet of snacks that was sticking out from one of the pockets.

'Ah, they're his favourite treats. So, what did he do?'

'It's been hilarious. First, he tried jumping straight up in the air to snatch it. But that didn't work. So then he tried balancing on that chair there, but it wouldn't hold his weight.'

I was laughing myself now.

'He came close once,' Steve said. 'He jumped off the table and managed to grab a hold of the side of the bag. He was hanging on for grim life with his claws. But he couldn't hold it and slipped back down again, like a cartoon character.'

I gave Bob a ruffle on the back of his neck.

'You never give up, do you, mate,' I said.

I then reached for the snacks from the rucksack and gave him a couple of treats.

Steve couldn't help smiling. He was something of a philosopher. Or liked to think he was, at least.

'They say that's the secret of life,' he said.

'What is?'

'Fall down seven times, get up eight.'

I smiled. He was right. We should never give in. Perseverance always pays off.

Trust Your Instincts

Bob and I were walking through the West End, on our way home after a meeting. I'd decided to head in the direction of our old 'pitch' on Neal Street, where my old friend Sam co-ordinated sales of *The Big Issue* to the area's small army of vendors. I hadn't seen her for a while and wanted to say hello.

We'd not been walking for long when Bob started getting agitated, turning around in circles on my shoulder and making a loud mewling sound.

I placed him down on the pavement and gave him a snack, then pressed on. He was still unhappy. I'd walked a couple of hundred yards down another street, when I saw a commotion on the corner ahead of me.

Black smoke was billowing into the air and I could hear fire-engine sirens drawing closer. There were already men in yellow coats cordoning off the area and tourists and shoppers were being hurriedly shepherded away from the scene.

It was obvious there was a major incident, a fire or perhaps worse, some kind of terrorist incident. So I put Bob on my shoulders and took a circuitous route back to the railway station, from where we would head home to Surrey.

Thankfully, I learned later from Sam that the incident was a small, household fire, caused by someone leaving their kitchen hob on. No one had been hurt. But it could easily have been something much worse. The incident stuck in my mind, because of the way Bob reacted.

Cats have highly developed senses that allow them to detect things that we humans cannot, such as earthquakes and major storms. They can also pick up on human illness, epilepsy in particular. Bob had intuitively picked up on something in the West End. Fortunately, my instinct had been to listen to him.

It reinforced something that I had long believed in. That we should all listen to our instincts, to our gut feelings. They are invariably right.

Change One Person's World

Bob and I were sitting in a doorway, taking shelter from the rain. It was literally bouncing off the pavement; there was little prospect of us selling any magazines.

But then, out of nowhere, we were approached by a very striking young lady. She was pretty with dark hair and was wearing a yellow raincoat.

Judging from her accent, she was Russian – or something like that. She leaned down and gave Bob a gentle ruffle on the back of the neck. I noticed that she was wearing a bracelet with an inscription in another language. I asked her what it meant.

She smiled. 'It's an expression from Estonia. Where I'm from. It says: Who does not thank for little, will not thank for much.'

'How true that is,' I said, smiling back.

She spent a few minutes with us, chatting quietly about nothing in particular. She gave me a couple of pounds for a magazine, before giving Bob a final nuzzle and heading off.

'Thank you,' she said.

I gave her a little hug.

'No, thank you,' I said.

The biggest impact can sometimes come from the smallest acts. What that lady did that evening was such a little thing. It took her only a few moments, but it meant a great deal to me. You don't have to change the whole world to help someone, sometimes it's enough to change that person's world for a few moments.

Find Your Bliss

When Bob and I were busking, I was always surprised at how relaxed he was, sitting amongst the crowds in Covent Garden and around Piccadilly.

On the rare occasion he did get agitated, there was something that was always liable to calm him down: music. As soon as I started strumming away at my guitar, his body language changed. He seemed more mellow. His tail-wagging fell into the distinctive, wind-screen-wiper pattern that indicated he was happy. That he had found his own form of bliss.

More recently, if I am recording music in my little studio at home, he has to sit directly behind me when the sound is booming out. No matter how loud it gets, and it can get very loud, he wants to be there.

Music has, at various times, been my own salvation. Seeing its impact on Bob has underlined to me that we all have something that has the power to soothe, restore and lift us when we need it.

We all need to find our bliss sometimes.

The Courage to Ask

I was sitting outside a coffee shop in Islington with Bob. It was a very hippyish place; inside the walls were covered in little bits of philosophy. Sayings, mantras. Little slices of wisdom.

One had jumped out at me as I'd ordered my coffee.

'Be strong enough to stand alone, smart enough to know when you need help and brave enough to ask for it.'

It made me think immediately of Bob.

When he'd been injured, he had managed to remove himself from the danger he faced and position himself in my block of flats. He had somehow worked out that it was his best chance of getting some help. As it turned out, his instincts had brought him to me.

Of course, his experience echoed my own. When I'd been homeless, I'd put myself in terrible danger. But I'd found the strength to remove myself, to recognise that I needed to beat my drug addiction and to seek out the treatment I needed.

These days, when I'm doing charity work, I am frequently asked to offer advice to addicts or homeless people who feel lost and unable to escape their fates. I often refer to that saying in the coffee shop.

At our lowest ebbs, we all need to find the strength to stand alone, the intelligence to know we need help – and, most of all, the courage to ask.

New Isn't Always Better

Bob's favourite toy for many years was his 'raggedy' mouse. It was a battered old fabric animal with buttons for eyes and a string tail. He loved tugging and tearing at it, flinging and flipping it around the room so that he could chase after it. After a while it became a tattered rag, a shapeless shadow of its former self, but he didn't care. Bob loved the thing. He could while away hours playing with it.

I tried replacing it a couple of times, swapping it for newer toys, but he didn't take an interest in any of them. Instead he stalked the flat looking for his old mouse. Once I put it in the bin, but even then he sniffed it out.

I was genuinely worried that it might be harmful to him, that the old fabric might be infected. And I was sure that he should have something newer, shinier, more exciting. But I was totally missing the point.

I was seeing things from my perspective. To me his raggedy mouse was a sad, broken thing. Fit only for the dustbin. But Bob saw it completely differently. It was his toy. It made him happy. It provided him with stimulation, entertainment and escape. He didn't need anything else. He kept it for years after that.

Everyone today is so obsessed with having the new version of everything. The latest version phone, laptop, video game, fashion item. But why? If they are doing their job, do we really need them? Is new necessarily better? If we stopped and thought about it, we'd probably be just as happy with what we already have.

Silver Linings

Working with Bob on the set of the movie about us was demanding work – and not only because we often had to get up at 5 a.m. in the morning to get to the set on time.

Unlike the 'professional' cats on the set, Bob wasn't trained to act for the cameras and would frequently do unpredictable things. Often, for instance, he would drop his head or turn around, when the cameramen wanted him to look directly into the lens.

I had to develop a repertoire of tricks and ploys to keep his eye-line where the cameraman needed it to be. I did everything from positioning myself behind the camera, clicking my fingers, to pointing a laser pen at the walls to make him look around the room.

It was inevitable that he wouldn't always stick to the script. But the director, Roger Spottiswoode, used Bob's odd moments of improvisation to good effect.

One day, rather than sitting still for the camera as required, Bob started chasing the laser pen around the room. Roger kept the cameras going and used the footage in another scene in which Bob is seen pursuing a mouse.

It was a reminder that life rarely goes exactly to plan. But we can always turn difficulties to our advantage. Every cloud has a silver lining, as they say. We should always look for that positive.

We All Have Something to Give

It was a week before Christmas and Bob and I were struggling to make ends meet during a spell of cold weather. We were busking near Shaftesbury Avenue one evening, when a Salvation Army band and choir arrived and began singing the Christmas carol, 'In the Bleak Midwinter.' I found myself drawn in by the words, in particular to the final verse:

146

What can I give Him, poor as I am?

If I were a shepherd, I would bring a
    lamb.

If I were a Wise Man, I would do my
    part;

Yet what I can I give Him: give my heart.

Times were hard and I suddenly felt
sorry for myself.

Ha, I thought. What do I have to give?
Nothing.

But I was wrong.

Just then a lady passed by. She was in
her fifties, smartly dressed, but looking a
little emotional.

'Would you mind if I had a moment with
him?' she said, seeing Bob. 'Of course,' I
replied.

As she sat and stroked Bob, we began
chatting. It turned out it was the anniver-
sary of her son's death. She was no longer

married to the boy's father and was heading home to an empty house. She'd had a cat, but it had died six months earlier, too.

'I'm dreading tonight,' she said, dabbing away a tear. 'I'll be all alone there with my memories. You are so lucky to have Bob here with you.'

It stopped me in my tracks. I felt such a fool.

We all have something to give. No matter how small or trivial we might think it is, it could mean the world to someone else. No matter how sorry we are feeling for ourselves, we should never forget it.

The Power of Hope

Bob seems to be able to lift and inspire people wherever we go. He has put smiles on faces, young and old. Moved many to tears. To be honest, it was hard for me to understand this at first. How could the story of a cat helping to transform the life of a troubled young man have touched so many people in so many parts of the world?

An encounter in Oslo, in Norway, shone a light.

Our publishers there had arranged for Bob to meet a lady called Anne. She was blind, but had read the Braille versions of our books and become one of our biggest fans in Norway.

She was beside herself with joy at meeting Bob, even though – obviously – she couldn't see him.

He doesn't always respond to being touched, especially in busy situations, but when she began stroking him, he reciprocated by rubbing his head against her. It was as if he sensed how important this moment was to her.

Through an interpreter, someone asked her what it was that had struck such a powerful chord in her. Her answer came down to one word: hope.

The hope she'd seen in the story of Bob and me had shone light in her darkness, she said. It had given her hope where, often, she'd not had very much at all. It was a simple answer. And a profound one, too. It made me realise that we all need to feel hope. And it doesn't matter where we see or find it.

We Are Not Alone

In 2017, Bob and I were fortunate enough to visit Tokyo to attend the Japanese premiere of the movie of *A Street Cat Named Bob*.

Away from all the glamour, the most affecting moment came when we were introduced to two *The Big Issue* sellers, Akira and

Shinzo. Shinzo had a cat, too, a stray that he had named Mi. He had been living a pretty simple existence, living off scraps of food and sleeping rough. He'd tried selling *The Big Issue*, but found it very hard going. He couldn't attract people's attention. Mi had changed his fortunes immediately.

'People were more open to me,' he said. 'They stopped and talked.'

Akira had a similar story. He had briefly found a cat abandoned in a park. He had looked after it for two weeks before it was reunited with its owner. In that fortnight, he'd started taking the cat with him to sell *The Big Issue* outside the main railway station, where he had his pitch.

'I was no longer invisible. You know how that feels?' he said to me.

'Yes, I do,' I nodded. I told him that it had only been when Bob had come into my life that people had 'seen' me.

It was as if I was looking into a mirror. We all think we are unique. That no one can have had it is as bad as us. That is wrong.

No matter how desperate your situation. No matter how isolated and alone you might feel, the truth is you aren't alone at all. There is someone out there just like you. Going through the same things. It needed Bob to take me to the other side of the world to show me that.

Never Waste a Second Chance

Bob and I were far from home, at a book signing in Berlin.

We'd been busy meeting people for about an hour, when I looked up into the long queue and was drawn to a face in the crowd. At first, I couldn't quite believe it. It can't be her, I told myself. What was she doing here in Germany? But as she drew closer and closer to the front of the line, I saw that it really was her. I don't want to identify her, so let's call her Hannah.

Around eight or nine years ago, Hannah's life had been as much of a mess as mine. She, too, had been homeless and addicted to heroin. We had often slept rough in the same places in London. I hadn't seen her since those dark days.

Now, to my utter amazement, here she was – standing in line in a bookshop in Berlin. We met up afterwards and caught up. She told me that she had left London and her past to make a new life for herself. She told me that she was clean and in a relationship. Her face positively glowed with health and happiness. We promised each other that we would see each other again. (And we did. I returned to Berlin afterwards to spend more time with her.)

It was only in the days and hours that followed, the significance of the moment hit home. Like Hannah, I know that the battle against addiction is a daily one. It doesn't go away. It never will. But we have both found hope. And we can see the way ahead. Many of those with whom we shared those dark and distant days on the street were not so fortunate. We were the lucky ones that got out alive.

We are all gifted second chances in life. But those chances are worthless, unless we learn from the mistakes we made first time around.

There But For the Grace of God . . .

We were walking through the West End one winter evening, when Bob started getting agitated. At first, I thought it was the cold weather, but then I realised we were being followed.

Like Bob, I'd developed a radar for this over the years. I turned and spotted the guy in the throng. He was a young, slightly built lad, with greasy hair and a rucksack on his back.

We needed to cut through a small alleyway to get to the station. We'd barely entered the narrow street, when Bob let out a loud, *whew* noise. The young guy had lurched at us, grabbing at my rucksack.

I'm quite capable of looking after myself – as is Bob. Between us we pushed him away. He ran off, but only made it a few yards before he tripped and fell to the ground. The kid hauled himself to his knees and started crying.

Rather than send him off, I sat with him for a few minutes, talking. I could see he was desperate. He'd run away from an abusive home in the north of England without a penny to his name. He hadn't had a decent night's sleep in a week and had barely eaten. I told him about the best shelters to go to and wrote down a couple of phone numbers for charities that I knew might help. I also gave him some money. It was the least I could do.

If there was one lesson I'd learned during my time sleeping rough, it was that life on the streets dehumanises people. The desperation, loneliness and lack of decent, human contact drags you down. And in the process, you lose all sense of yourself – of what's right and wrong. It had happened to me.

In fact, I could see my younger self in this lad.

We are all too quick to rush to judgment. We all forget that, with a tiny twist of fate, any one of us could find ourselves on the street.

There, but for the grace of God, go all of us.

Don't Forget Where You Came From

Bob and I were approaching the end of a big book signing in London. We'd been meeting and greeting people for three hours and there was still a huge queue snaking around the store.

The managers of the bookshop had decided that they couldn't let any more people in. Reluctantly, I'd agreed to let them stop anyone else joining the line.

As usual, I had a couple of trusty friends helping me. One of them came in looking concerned. 'There's a mother and daughter here who caught the train down this morning from Glasgow. The train got delayed and they've just got here. They've been told they can't meet you and Bob. They're really upset.'

'Tell them to hang around,' I whispered in his ear.

At the end of the signing, the friend led them over. I let them sit down and stroke Bob for a minute while we chatted. I'd expected him to be exhausted by the end of a marathon signing, but he was as good as gold with them.

'We're so grateful,' the daughter said as, eventually, I told them we'd have to head off. 'It's Mum's birthday.'

I smiled.

'I think you've got it wrong there,' I said, giving the mother a hug. 'It's me who should be grateful. Without people like you, I'd never have made it off the streets.'

We're all guilty of forgetting our origins sometimes. But we shouldn't ever forget how we got to where we are in our lives

– and to be thankful to those who helped us get there.

Let Life Surprise You

To say that the recent transformation in my life was a surprise would be the understatement of the century. Never in a million years would I have imagined I'd be approached to write a book about my friendship with Bob. Never in a million years would I have anticipated that it would become a bestseller around the world.

And if I had told anyone that it would be turned into a movie, and premiered in the West End with Bob and I being introduced to the future Queen of England beforehand, then quite rightly, they would have thought I was utterly insane. Yet it did happen.

It's been said that wisdom is the ability to learn from change. Well, if I haven't acquired some wisdom – some perspective – from the massive changes that have occurred in my life, there is little hope for me. One of the simplest things I've learned is that sometimes you have to let fate play its hand.

Sometimes the best things happen unexpectedly. For seemingly no reason at all. There's nothing you can do about it. So the best thing you can do is just let go.

Let go – and let life surprise you.

Money Can't Buy You Love

Bob and I were sitting in a very swanky hotel room in Tokyo. It had been a busy day and I'd treated us to a really nice dinner, on room service: a delicious steak for me and

160

gourmet chicken cat food for Bob. It truly was five-star luxury.

As I sat there enjoying my meal, I couldn't help but think back over our time together and other, much less fancy meals we'd had. I remembered the first night that we'd gone busking together in Covent Garden and how, thanks to Bob's charisma, I'd earned two or three times what I would normally have earned. I'd treated myself to a curry and him to a tin of tuna. Back then I'd been used to eating from tins. Or living simply off breakfast cereal.

So what was different tonight? The truth was, nothing really. Yes, the food was being served on fine china and the wine was a very good vintage. But certainly as far as Bob was concerned, it didn't matter.

To Bob it was of absolutely no significance whether we were in a five-star hotel or a fifth-floor flat. It didn't matter whether I had fifty pence or fifty pounds in my pocket.

Money, wealth, whatever you want to call it, is a transient thing. It comes and it goes. We all go through periods of feast and famine. Times when we feel – financially, at least – rich and poor. But that is only ever part of the picture.

Money doesn't give us the most important things of all in life. It certainly doesn't buy us love.

As we ate like kings in our Tokyo suite, I gave Bob a little ruffle. Even if I was to end up back on the street, I would still be a rich man.

As long as I had him with me.

Acknowledgements

I coudn't possibly let a book like this end without drawing on another piece of wisdom that I've picked up during my time with Bob: the importance of saying thank you. It's been six years now since my first, tentative steps into the world of publishing. Back in 2012, when *A Street Cat Named Bob* was first published, I was more than a little daunted by it all. But now – half a dozen books later – each new project seems like a reunion with old and trusted friends. That's certainly the case with Rowena Webb, my publisher at Hodder and Stoughton, who first took me on all those years ago and whose idea has now provided the spark for this book. She therefore must get my first thanks. I'd also like to single out Kerry Hood, Rosie Stephen, Ian Wong and the rest of the talented team at Hodder, as well as Dan Williams for his adorable illustrations. Thanks must also go to my agent Lesley Thorne and everyone at Aitken Alexander for all the work they do on my behalf. I really appreciate it. Last – but definitely not least – I must again thank Garry Jenkins, who has been on this journey the longest of all, since Bob and I first met him on a wintry day outside the Angel, Islington in December 2010, in fact. Somehow, he always manages to find the right words – although, I suspect, even he probably doesn't have enough of them to sum up the debt of gratitude I owe him. So I'll end where I began, by just saying thank you.

THE LITTLE BOOK OF BOB

To find out more about James
and Bob, visit their website at

www.streetcatbob.world

You can also follow them on Twitter
at www.twitter.com/streetcatbob,
or visit their Facebook page at
www.facebook.com/streetcatbob for
the latest news, stories and pictures.

How to make your Felicity wishes

W I S H

With this book comes an extra special wish
for you and your best friend.

Hold the book together at each end and
both close your eyes.

Wriggle your noses and think of a
number under ten.

Open your eyes, whisper the numbers you
thought of to each other.

Add these numbers together. This is your

Magic Number.

you

best friend

Place your little finger
on the stars, and say your magic number
out loud together. Now make your wish
quietly to yourselves. And maybe, one day,
your wish might just come true.

Love *felicity* X

With sparkly wishes for Alice Thompson,
with love Auntie Emma x

First published in Great Britain in 2006 by Hodder Children's Books

The right of Emma Thomson to be identified as the author and illustrator of this work has been asserted by her in accordance with the Copyright, Designs and Patents Act 1988.

2

A Catalogue record for this book is available from the British Library

ISBN: 978 0 340 91826 5

Printed in the UK by CPI Bookmarque, Croydon, CR0 4TD

The paper and board used in this paperback by Hodder Children's Books are natural recyclable products made from wood grown in sustainable forests. The manufacturing processes conform to the environmental regulations of the country of origin.

Hodder Children's Books
A division of Hachette Children's Books, 338 Euston Road, London NW1 3BH
An Hachette Livre UK Company

Emma Thomson's felicity Wishes®

Holly's Hideaway
and other stories

CONTENTS

Shopping Surprise

Holly wasn't a natural fairy. She had to work hard at doing all the things a good fairy should. It wasn't that she didn't want to be a good fairy, although she did sometimes struggle with the effort it took!

But there was one aspect of being a fairy that Holly excelled in – fashion!

Holly was the trendiest fairy in the whole of Little Blossoming. She was always ahead of the latest fashions, always had the most up-to-date wardrobe, and always, always looked amazing!

And it was no secret that Holly wanted to be a Christmas Tree Fairy when she graduated. She loved to be the centre of attention – and sitting on top of a tree looking pretty would certainly be suited to her idle nature!

"What do you mean, you've forgotten your flying wings?" said Miss Speeding, the school flying mistress.

"They're so uncomfortable," moaned Holly, who was not especially bothered about learning to loop the loop. "Can't I fly in these instead?" She spun round and showed Miss Speeding the top fairy fashion accessory of the moment.

"You know perfectly well, Holly, that those wings are not for professional flying. These flimsy things may look lovely," she tapped them disapprovingly

with her wand, "but practical they
are not. I'm surprised you even made
it into school this morning without
falling from the sky."

Holly quickly covered her dirty
knees with her bag. The last thing
she wanted was for Miss Speeding to
know that she had indeed fallen from
the sky that morning.

9

Miss Speeding looked thoughtful for a moment and, without another word, headed back to her office.

"I think I've got out of the flying lesson!" said Holly gleefully to Felicity. "I should forget my flying wings more often!"

Felicity shook her head. "I can't believe you want to get out of it. It's the most amazing fairy feeling in the world, being able to swoop and fly like a bird."

"Oh, I like flying, I just don't like all the physical exertion and getting all hot and bothered," said Holly, who'd always been more than a little lazy. "It always ruins my hairdo."

"Right!" said Miss Speeding, returning to address Holly.

"I've got some homework I can be getting on with until the flying class is finished," offered Holly.

"Oh, there'll be no need for that,"

said Miss Speeding. "I found you these."
And from behind her back Miss
Speeding produced the most horrid,
ugly old wings Holly had ever seen!

"Chop, chop!" said Miss Speeding. "Don't stand there gawping. Get changed quickly and then fly and join the others on the right wing of the school roof."

Felicity stared at the tatty old wings and then at her fashion-conscious friend. "Don't worry, Holly. I'm sure it will be fine," she said, trying to sound confident.

* * *

Two days later, Holly still hadn't got over the indignity of it. She was one of those fairies who was very concerned about what everyone else thought.

"You're going to have to take off those dark glasses at some time or other," said Felicity, disconcerted at not being able to see her friend's eyes.

"I can't," sobbed Holly. "I'm too embarrassed. No one's ever going to forget what a fool I looked in flying class on Monday."

"Oh, Holly," said Polly. "You're exaggerating. No one even noticed your wings in flying class."

"What wings?" asked Daisy, trying to make her friend feel better.

But just as she said it two novice fairies from the year below walked past the fairy friends, pointed at Holly and then started to giggle uncontrollably.

"You were saying?" said Holly,
distraught.

✳ ✳ ✳

Felicity didn't know what to say.
Instead, she started thinking. She
thought so hard and for so long that
it wasn't until lunchtime the next day
that she finally caught up with Holly
underneath the Large Oak Tree in the
middle of the playing field.

"I don't know how to say this without hurting your feelings," began Felicity, determined to be as honest as she could.

"Well, maybe you shouldn't say anything," said Holly, who was sure other fairies were still laughing at her.

"I just want to help," offered Felicity. "Look," she said softly, peeping over her friend's sunglasses, "I think sometimes you worry too much about what other fairies think. The most important thing is what you think on the inside. Do you understand what I mean?"

Holly didn't. All she knew was that she felt a fool and nothing she could imagine would change that.

"I've had an idea," said Felicity. "It's going to be hard. But you are the only fairy I know who can make it work."

Holly sighed. She knew Felicity's

ideas didn't always go to plan. Short of Felicity turning her into another fairy or giving her a one-way ticket to another country halfway around Fairy World, Holly couldn't think of anything that could make her feel better.

"Will it make the giggling and teasing stop?" she asked.

"It will!" said Felicity, resolutely.

Holly looked unconvinced. "Don't tell me. You've made a sparkledust concoction in chemistry to make everyone in school forget they saw the trendiest fairy in Little Blossoming looking like a walking dustbin!"

Felicity winced. "No," she said patiently. "It's not sparkledust exactly. But it is a magic wish. And for you to make it work you're going to have to use your best acting skills."

"Acting skills?" said Holly. She took off her glasses and swished her hair dramatically. "I've always loved drama, you know that."

In the blink of an eye, Holly slipped into the role she'd played in the school pantomime – Cinderella. Felicity giggled as Holly pretended to sweep the floor around her and wipe her tired brow.

"What's the role?" asked Holly, coming back to reality.

Felicity paused. "The role is the most demanding one you've ever done!" she said, rummaging around in her bag. "I'd like you to wear these all day, every day for seven days and nights… and love it!"

And Felicity pulled out the horrid old wings Miss Speeding had made Holly wear in flying class just a few days before.

"Are you crazy?" said Holly, thinking it was some kind of joke.

"I said it would be a demanding role!"

said Felicity. "Just think how much acting talent it will take to pull it off convincingly!"

Holly was aghast that her friend actually seemed to be serious.

"But of course," said Felicity, "if you don't think you're talented enough…"

"Talented?" said Holly. "You know I'm the best fairy at drama in the whole school!"

"Then you should have no problem doing this," said Felicity, holding out the wings.

Holly poked them with the end of her wand, a disgusted look on her face. "I don't see what possible good it would do except to make people laugh at me even more."

"Well," said Felicity, taking Holly's sparkling trendy wings off her and handing her the old tatty ones, "that depends. If you're as good an actress as you think you are then I can guarantee something magical will happen."

Holly still looked unsure.

"Trust me," said Felicity. "I'm a fairy!"

* * *

Holly had nothing to lose. She knew that she couldn't carry on hiding behind dark glasses for ever, and she knew that she could trust Felicity to have her best interests at heart.

With a heavy sigh, Holly pulled on the horrid wings as though they were the most beautiful, exclusive pair of wings she had ever owned. She straightened her shoulders, beamed an enormous smile, and winked at Felicity.

"All the best actresses are true professionals," she called out as she flew into school with her head held high.

Just as Felicity had warned, it was the hardest role Holly had ever had to play. Harder than the time she'd acted the lead in the school Christmas play, harder than the time she'd gone on at the last minute in the talent competition... and even harder than the time she'd had to tell a white lie to Fairy Godmother to get her friends out of trouble.

* * *

"Nice wings!" giggled Daisy and Winnie as Holly sat down beside them in class.

"Yes," said Holly, to the surprise of everyone watching. "They are, aren't they! After Miss Speeding made me wear them the other day I realized they were actually far more practical than the usual silly fashion nonsense I wear."

"You can't be serious," said Polly, who had fluttered over from the other side of the room. "They're horrid, and full of holes!"

"I'm perfectly serious," said Holly, loudly. "They may have holes, but

21

they certainly have more character than the wings everyone gets from 'Wings and Things'. No one else in the school has a pair of wings like these!" she said with pride, getting up on to her chair and spinning around on the spot for the whole class to see.

Felicity beamed at her friend. Holly really was a great actress.

"Oh," said Polly. "I thought you were wearing them for a joke or something."

"No joke!" said Holly, as she watched her acting skills convince the fairies around her. "These wings are currently my favourite accessory!"

✳ ✳ ✳

As the week progressed, Felicity watched from the sidelines as fairies' attitudes towards Holly and her wings changed. She was standing close to a couple of novice fairies at break-time when she heard them discussing her friend.

"I always thought she was so into her looks!" said one fairy.

"I know. She was always so perfect-looking in the latest fashions, and I was too afraid to speak to her. I never felt trendy enough to be her friend," said the other fairy. "But she's normal. Just like the rest of us!"

Felicity smiled. Her secret plan was working.

* * *

When Felicity met up with Holly to fly home from school at the end of the week, Holly was back to her normal self. In fact, Felicity thought that Holly was more herself then she had ever been. The sensitive side that Holly normally hid with her fashionable clothes was there for everyone to see, not just her closest friends.

"It's so good to see you happy and yourself again. I hope this part isn't acting!" said Felicity. "It's day six. Only one more day to go and the magic will have worked completely."

"You know," said Holly, "I only had to act for the first two hours, which were definitely the worst. But after that, wearing these funny wings just felt like normal. The magic worked quicker than you thought!"

Felicity smiled. "You're not telling me that you're going to carry on wearing those wings after the seven days and seven nights are up?"

"Oh, goodness no," said Holly. "Much as I've grown attached to the flying performance of these wings, I won't miss them when they've gone!"

∗ ∗ ∗

By the final day of Holly's magical task, she had come to understand what Felicity had tried to explain the previous week. Because she was being herself and not relying on how she looked to win attention and friends, Holly had actually ended up with more friends and attention than she'd ever had before.

The most magical thing, though, had happened on the inside. Holly had realized that it didn't matter what she wore; she was still the same fairy underneath.

∗ ∗ ∗

When Holly arrived outside

registration to join her friends the next day, there were surprises in store for everyone.

"I see you've got your sparkling wings back on again!" said Polly, immediately noticing the change in her friend.

"The old wings were great for a while," said Holly, putting down her school bag. She was telling the truth. "But I thought it was time to tidy up my appearance."

"I think you might change your mind when you see the rest of the class," said Daisy, as she pushed open the door to a roomful of fairies… all wearing holey old wings!

"I think you've started a new craze!" said Felicity, giggling. "That magic was stronger than I thought!"

"And stronger than you'd ever believe!" said Holly as she slipped off her coat to reveal a holey old dress that even Felicity would have sent to the charity shop years ago.

"It's called shabby chic!" said Holly. "Haven't you heard? It's the latest thing!"

Holly's Hideaway

"Describe your friend in three words," read out Felicity Wishes from her *Fairy Girl* magazine. She was sitting in Sparkles café with Winnie, Daisy and Polly – and Holly, who had just burst in with a dramatic entrance.

"Oh, where do you begin?" gasped Holly. "Just three! It's impossible."

"Dramatic!" called out Polly, as Holly swished her hair.

"Confident!" shouted Winnie as

Holly spun round to flare out her dress.

"Loud!" said Daisy, even louder than Holly would have.

"Is that it?" asked Holly, looking round at her friends for more. "What about beautiful, elegant, intelligent, charming..."

Felicity, Polly, Winnie and Daisy fell about laughing.

"Well, you're certainly not shy and quiet!" said Felicity.

Holly was bursting with news! Her shabby chic look had really taken off across Fairy World. Fairies everywhere wanted to know where they could buy shabby chic, fashion designers copied the style, and now Holly had been asked to do a photoshoot for *Fairy Girl* magazine! She couldn't wait another minute to tell her friends.

Felicity jumped up and gave Holly a big hug. "That's brilliant, Hol! Just think, a whole article all about you and your clothes. You'll be the star of Little Blossoming."

"But it's not just about me," said Holly, beaming. They want to capture the spirit of fairy friendship in the article too, so you're all invited to the photoshoot!"

Whoops and cheers filled the café as the fairy friends pretended to walk along a catwalk, striking poses and weaving in and out of shocked fairies sitting with their milkshakes.

"Oh, my goodness!" exclaimed Daisy, once they'd collapsed back down on the comfy sofa. "When is it happening?"

"Tomorrow!" said Holly.

"Tomorrow! But we'll never be ready on time!" cried Daisy. "I have nothing shabby chic to wear other than my gardening clothes – and I'm pretty sure that they're more shabby than chic!"

"Don't worry," said Felicity. "If we set off now we've got all day to shop for new outfits. I hear Miss Fairy in Bloomfield has just had a delivery of the latest shabby chic designs."

"Well, I already know what I'm wearing," said Holly, "so I'm off to the hairdresser's for a sparkling cut to go with my new look!"

"Lets meet back here at 4 p.m. then, Miss Dramatic, Confident and Loud!" called out Felicity as she waved to Holly.

"OK," giggled Holly. "See you all then!"

* * *

Holly had been going to Fairy Hair for as long as she could remember. She always had the same fairy cut her hair. Sarah knew exactly how to cut Holly's hair so that she loved it every time.

Holly adored going to the hairdresser's. It always made her feel so special. From sitting reading the magazines, to the head massage when her hair was washed, to the gossip she shared with Sarah and no one else! The best bit, though, was leaving the hairdresser's on a little cloud, looking and feeling fantastic and watching the reactions of passing fairies on the street.

But today wasn't Holly's lucky day. When she got to Fairy Hair, the receptionist told her that Sarah wasn't feeling very well and had gone home. Holly was crushed. She had to be looking her best for the photoshoot the next day!

"Don't worry," said the receptionist. "This is Lola. She's available to cut your hair instead."

Holly looked up at Lola. She looked very nice and had a fantastic haircut herself.

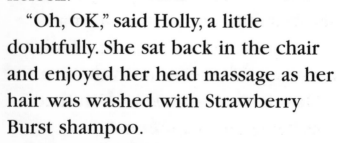

"Oh, OK," said Holly, a little doubtfully. She sat back in the chair and enjoyed her head massage as her hair was washed with Strawberry Burst shampoo.

Lola was lovely. But it wasn't the same as having Sarah.

"Right," Lola said, sitting Holly in

front of the mirror. "What can I do for you?"

"Just the usual," said Holly, unhelpfully.

"Sorry," said Lola, "but I don't know what 'the usual' is!"

"Just a trim, so my hair doesn't get in my eyes. And a fantastic big-hair blow dry so everyone in the street notices me!"

Lola was looking thoughtfully at Holly in the mirror. "You know," she said, "I think you'd look great with curly blonde hair!"

Holly frowned. "Really? My hair's always been straight and brown."

Lola pulled out a magazine with a famous fashion fairy on the cover.

"Just look at Sally Silver!" gushed Lola. "Isn't she glamorous?"

"Yes," said Holly dreamily. "But I could never look like her."

Lola bundled all Holly's hair up in

a big clip and dragged a few strands down across her face. "Oh, yes you could! I bet you'd look even better!"

Holly tried to peer at herself in the mirror through the hair that Lola had pulled across her eyes. She couldn't see it, no matter how hard she tried.

"No," she said, "I'll stick with just the trim and blow dry."

Lola sighed disappointedly. "You're probably right. You need to be a very loud, dramatic and confident person to pull off a look like that."

"But I am that kind of person!" burst out Holly "All my friends say so!"

"Then you should have this hairstyle!" said Lola, tapping the magazine with her comb.

"Well," said Holly resolutely, "I think I will!"

* * *

While Holly was at the hairdresser's having her makeover, Felicity, Polly, Daisy and Winnie spent the afternoon desperately trying to find outfits for the photoshoot. Felicity tried on every

ragged skirt in the shop,
but they were all too long
for her and she kept
tripping over the hems.
Daisy tried on a floppy,
flowery hat,
but she
couldn't
see properly and knocked
over a stand of bags. And
when Winnie and Polly
tried on their outfits, they
were sure they looked more
like fairy scarecrows
than shabby chic!
"This is hopeless!"
sighed Winnie.
"We're not going
to have anything
to wear for the photoshoot."
Just then there was a ring
at the door and a Delivery
Fairy walked in with a bundle

of the latest shabby chic dresses hot off the catwalk – and there was even one in pink, perfect for Felicity. It wasn't long before the fairies' frowns turned into beams as they swished and twirled in their fabulous new outfits.

"Come on, let's go and show Holly our new dresses," said Felicity, skipping out of the shop door.

* * *

Holly had never had so many treatments on her hair at once! First Lola had chosen three different shades of blonde to dye her hair, "for a more natural look". She'd applied it to every strand of hair with a little brush, then wrapped the hair in little packages of silver foil. Then she'd pulled out one hundred small round curlers, sprinkled them with sparkledust and wound the silver packages round them. Next she got an enormous head-warmer on wheels and pulled it down over Holly's head.

"There," she said, twisting a timer on the back. "I'll leave you to cook for an hour and when I come back we'll wash it out and see the results."

It was 3 p.m. already and Holly knew she was going to be late to meet her friends. So she was relieved to see her friends' faces appear at the window of Fairy Hair, and waved frantically for them to come in.

The fairies stared at their friend. Holly looked quite something under her layers of tin foil! There were no hairdressers to be seen.

"I'm so glad you're here!" whispered Holly. "I let myself be talked into a new haircut, but I'm really not sure about it. They've even dyed my eyebrows!"

Daisy couldn't help but stare at the blonde curls that were peeping out of the tin foil.

"Erm… don't worry!" said Felicity, trying to sound encouraging. "You'll look great – you always do!"

✳ ✳ ✳

Lola wanted the new haircut to be a surprise to Holly, so only Felicity, Polly, Daisy and Winnie could see it being slowly revealed as Lola made the finishing touches. Holly couldn't tell anything from her friends' faces, but her hairdresser was grinning wildly.

"The moment of truth, Holly!" she said. "Or should I say Sally Silver?"

Holly didn't hear. She was staring

in shock at the fairy that looked at
her in the mirror. She was hoping that
it was all a very strange dream. But
there was a part of her that knew that
wasn't going to be the case. Instead
of her straight brown hair she now
had bouncing blonde curls. She didn't
know whether she liked it or not, but

it was certainly very, very different from what she was used to.

Polly, Daisy and Winnie didn't know what to say. They were completely speechless.

"You look… erm… amazing!" said Felicity, trying to break the silence. She hardly recognized her friend. Holly just didn't look like Holly any more!

* * *

Even when Lola waved goodbye outside Fairy Hair, Holly was still in a dreamlike state. She wasn't on the usual cloud of happiness that normally lifted her step as she walked down the street. And it wasn't that fairies weren't stopping and staring at her hair. Felicity thought more fairies were looking at Holly than ever before. But although Holly usually loved attention, somehow it didn't feel real. All she wanted to do was hide.

Holly couldn't get home quickly enough. Felicity and her friends did their best to help. But when Holly caught sight of herself in her hall mirror, she moaned and ran to throw herself face first on her bed.

Felicity couldn't bear to see her friend like this. She had to get Holly back on track for the photoshoot. And there was only one fairy she knew who could save the day…

* * *

When Holly woke the next morning she thought for one blissful moment that the previous day had been a terrible nightmare. As she lay looking at the chink of light that burst through the curtains she smiled to herself. What a silly dream! She'd never in a million fairy years agree to have her gorgeous brown locks chopped and changed.

But then a blond curl fell into her eyes and she realized her nightmare

46

was real. She lay back in bed with a loud groan. She couldn't go to the photoshoot feeling like someone she wasn't! She'd just have to hide away in her room until her curls fell out and her own hair grew back!

At that moment there was a ring at the front door, but Holly didn't move from under the duvet. She was safe in her cosy hideaway! But the next thing she knew, there was a soft knock on her bedroom door and Felicity peeped in.

"There's someone very special to see you, Holly!" she whispered.

Holly was surprised: her friend was never one for early mornings! But she knew she had to put Felicity off somehow. "I'm sorry, Felicity, I really don't want to see anyone," croaked Holly. "I'm... I'm not feeling very well. I don't think I'll be able to go to the photoshoot."

But another face peeped round the door. The last person Holly was expecting. It was Sarah from Fairy Hair!

* * *

An hour later, Holly was sitting in her kitchen with Sarah, surrounded by clouds of sparkledust. Sarah was putting Holly's hair back just the way she liked it!

"Felicity came round to my house last night," explained Sarah. "I hadn't been feeling very well, but she really cheered me up when she told me all about your shabby chic look taking over the fashion world. And when she told me about your new hairdo and the photoshoot, I knew I had to come and help!"

"I was so worried about you," added Felicity. "You did look like Sally Silver, but you didn't look like yourself! And you'd lost all the dramatic, loud, confidence that makes you you. I almost didn't recognize you! I knew Sarah was a good friend of yours, and I was sure she'd come to the rescue."

"Felicity, you're the best friend a fairy could wish for!" said Holly, grinning from ear to ear as she saw her new hair in the mirror. "We're going to wow them at *Fairy Girl*!"

✷ ✷ ✷

The fairy friends had never had as much fun as they did that day! They twirled, posed, preened and pouted to the cameras, giggling hysterically and showing the cameras what friends are really for. Even Sarah borrowed

one of Holly's outfits and came along too! Felicity, Polly, Winnie, Daisy and Sarah were stunning in their shabby chic. But Holly stole the show, swishing her brown locks in her old confident way.

The fairies at *Fairy Girl* magazine said that it was one of the best photoshoots they'd ever done.

"That was brilliant!" Holly burst out as the fairy friends left the studio.

"I can't wait to see next week's magazine, with us in it!" cried Winnie. "We're going to be famous!"

"Only one thing," added Holly. "I realized that I never asked Sarah to dye my eyebrows back to their old colour. They're still a little bit blonde!"

"Leave them," said Felicity. "You're a true individual, and beautiful just the way you are!"

Musical Moments

Holly was often misunderstood. Her extravagant nature and passion for fashionable clothes sometimes made her appear to other fairies as though she was attention-seeking and even a little bossy. But underneath Holly's bossiness was hidden a very sensitive side. A side that even her closest friends lost sight of now and then.

The School of Nine Wishes was preparing for the end of term musical – *The Sound of Fairies*. Felicity Wishes and her fairy friends were learning their lines and dance routines, making sets for the stage, finding props, and trying on their costumes.

✳ ✳ ✳

"Telling people what to do is all part of being dramatic!" Holly told Daisy, who was always exceptionally dreamy and quiet. "On the stage there's no room for being polite, waiting for people to do what they want when they want. You have to take charge or the show will never go on!"

Daisy felt awkward. For some inexplicable reason Fairy Godmother had chosen her to direct the end of term musical. It was a role that would have been much better suited to Holly, who was naturally dramatic and commanding and loved applause and attention.

But worse still, Fairy Godmother had insisted that Holly, who usually had the starring role in all the school plays and performances, gave someone else a chance. This year Holly would have a non-speaking, non-singing, dancing-only role in the chorus line with everyone else. It was proving very hard for Daisy, Holly and the rest of the cast, especially the fairy in the leading role...

✳ ✳ ✳

"I have no idea why Fairy Godmother chose me to be the star of the show," said Polly.

Holly winced as Polly said the word "star". Much as she loved her friend, she was finding it very difficult to be pleased for her. Holly was always the star. In her eyes there was only ever room for one fairy to shine the brightest. And she was the one!

"You're very good at learning lines," said Winnie, wanting Polly to have confidence in herself.

"And you always get top marks in

everything," said Daisy. "Maybe you'll
get top marks in this too!"

"I don't think so," said Polly. "I don't
have as much stage presence as Holly,"
she said truthfully.

Holly blushed and fanned herself with the flattery.

"You can learn to have presence," said Felicity. She saw Holly raise her eyebrows.

"Well," said Felicity, trying to take into account both her friends' feelings. "You can do your best to have presence, Polly, and," she added with a sudden brainwave, "Holly can teach you!"

Holly nearly dropped her wand.

"With all due respect, Polly," said Holly, "having stage presence isn't something you can teach. It's a magical ability that you have inside. Just like Daisy has a magical ability with flowers and Felicity has the magical ability to make friends."

"I see," said Felicity, who knew the way to Holly's heart. "So only the most accomplished fairies could ever hope to teach others what comes naturally to them?"

But Holly wasn't falling for Felicity's appeal to her vanity.

"No," said Holly patiently. "No one can ever teach a natural ability, even the professionals. You either have it or you don't."

"So, it's not that you don't want to teach Polly to be the best she can be in the starring role, it's just that you can't," continued Felicity, not giving up.

Holly sort of nodded, but realized that much as she didn't want to admit it, she didn't really want to help Polly. If she couldn't be the star of the show, a little piece of her didn't want anyone else to either, even if that anyone else was one of her best friends.

* * *

Holly only lasted through one terrible rehearsal before she gave in to the magic Felicity had started, and took Polly to one side.

"I know the other day I said it was impossible to teach someone stage presence," whispered Holly bravely, "but I've been thinking about what Felicity said. There are some technical pointers I could give you that might help you with your performance."

Polly looked dumbstruck. She knew how hard it was for Holly to offer her most treasured secrets.

"That's if you'd like some help," said Holly, unusually flustered. "I'm not saying that your performance is bad or anything, it's just…"

"Oh, no," said Polly. "I understand, and I'd be honoured. If you're sure you really wouldn't mind."

"I wouldn't mind at all," said Holly

resolutely. "As long as you promise me one thing."

"Anything," said Polly, who wanted the play to be a success.

"Don't tell anyone," said Holly, looking sheepish.

Polly nodded. "Of course," she said.

* * *

From that rehearsal on, Polly's performance improved dramatically!

"Well done!" said Daisy who was encouraged in her own directing ability when she saw how fantastic Polly had become in her star role. "When you spoke your lines before I could hardly hear you at the back of the hall. Now, your voice carries all over the school! I'd be surprised if they couldn't hear you in the canteen! It's like magic."

"Thanks," called Polly from the stage. "I suppose it is a kind of magic really, a secret magic," she said, looking around for Holly, who was nowhere to be seen.

"Right," said Daisy. "Time for Felicity's solo," she said, flipping the pages of her script. "Felicity?" she called out.

"Felicity!"

"Felicity!"

"Felicity!" echoed three different fairy voices from behind the scenes.

But Felicity didn't appear. She was busy in a secret meeting with Holly.

✳ ✳ ✳

"I can't thank you enough for helping me out like this," said Felicity, giving her friend a hug.

"I know you'd help me out if it was the other way round," said Holly, hugging her back. "It's the least a friend can do."

"Without all your secret professional top tips about singing to a large audience, my performance wouldn't be half as good," Felicity admitted. "I just don't understand why you insist that I don't tell anyone you've been helping me."

Holly blushed. She couldn't deny that Felicity's solo song had been pretty dreadful until she'd offered to coach her.

"Oh, listen!" said Felicity, hearing her name called. "I think it's time for me to go on."

And she dashed off in the direction of the stage.

* * *

"You must take time to learn your own role too," said Daisy to Holly

that evening as they sat on her sofa
surrounded by pages of script.

"There's not much to learn," said
Holly. "I could do it with my eyes
closed and no wings! It's much more
important that I spend time helping
you to become the best musical
director the School of Nine Wishes
has ever seen."

Holly had sat with Daisy for three hours that afternoon after school, as she had done every night for the last few weeks. With all her acting experience, Holly was able to help Daisy make notes on when and where people should enter and exit the stage. She helped her work out where they should stand to get the most from their voice and she showed her how to improve on the cast's strengths while she secretly helped them with their weaknesses.

"Fairy Godmother congratulated me today on how the musical was coming on," said Daisy, awkwardly.

"That's great," said Holly, beaming. "It's looking really fantastic."

"I know!" said Daisy. "Somehow, magically, it's all coming together. Winnie's dance routine has improved enormously, Felicity's singing is suddenly fantastic and Polly's starring role… what can I say? I'd never thought anyone could be half as good as you, but she's got this confidence and ability from nowhere. It's amazing."

Holly blushed with her secret.

"If only you'd let me tell Fairy Godmother how much you've helped me," said Daisy. "When she congratulated me, I felt a bit of a fake taking all the credit."

"Don't be silly," said Holly. "I may have been helping you, but you've done all the hard work and really pulled this show together. The biggest credit I could hope for is that the show is a huge success. That's all that matters."

Holly could hardly believe what she was hearing herself say. Only a few weeks ago the most important thing to her would have been standing in the middle of the stage and getting all the applause herself.

✳ ✳ ✳

At last it was the night before the first performance and Holly was feeling strange. She had a feeling in her tummy she hadn't felt for years. Butterflies!

"You look dreadful!" said Felicity, when she saw her usually preened friend with bags under her eyes.

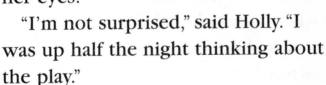

"I'm not surprised," said Holly. "I was up half the night thinking about the play."

"Are you worried about your role?" asked Felicity.

"Oh, no, no!" said Holly. "I haven't even looked at it yet! I haven't had butterflies about performing myself for ages. I've got so used to getting up on stage it doesn't bother me any more."

"So, what are you worried about then?" asked Felicity, confused.

"I've been thinking about you, Daisy, Polly and Winnie. I really want you all to be as brilliant as I know you can be. I want this musical to be the biggest success the School of Nine Wishes has ever seen!"

* * *

Finally, it was time. There wasn't an empty seat in the audience. The lights went down, the curtain went up and the musical show began.

Winnie was wonderful, Felicity was fantastic and Polly was perfect. The final scene used every fairy in the

entire cast to fill the stage with an
amazing, revolving dance routine.
It wasn't a particularly complicated
dance, but the effect was brilliant.
Each fairy had to twist and turn and
pass under an arch in perfect time,
narrowly missing the other fairies.

As the dozens of fairies filed on to the stage, the tired Holly was already in a mess. Because she had been so confident that she could do the part without any practice, and because she had spent so much time helping her friends, Holly hadn't attended a single dress rehearsal. It was only in the last five minutes that she'd realized her costume didn't fit! As she staggered on to the stage in tights halfway up her legs and only one arm in her dress Holly was suddenly aware that she had no idea what was going on.

As she bumped and tripped into the centre she pulled six or so other fairies with her and together they crashed in a heap.

Remembering all the things Holly had taught her, Daisy immediately improvised. With her new-found directing skill she hastily ordered the stage hands to pull set screens in front of the flailing fairies even before the audience had time to notice. And within seconds she had instructed Felicity to repeat her solo while Polly and Winnie danced beside her. The effect was breathtaking and made even better when the screens pulled back to reveal the dance routine working just as it should.

The audience applauded so loudly
and for so long that the cast had to
return to the stage three times to take
a bow!

Holly nearly cried with pride and
relief.

* * *

Fairy Godmother, however, hadn't
seemed so impressed. On Monday
morning at school she summoned
Holly, Felicity, Polly, Daisy and Winnie
to her office.

"I'm sorry," said Holly, speaking
before Fairy Godmother had a chance.

"Oh, Holly," said Fairy Godmother.
"You have nothing to be sorry for. I
have asked you here to congratulate
you. The secret challenge I set you
was a hard one."

Holly frowned. "Secret challenge?"

Fairy Godmother nodded and
motioned for the fairies to sit down.

"Your dramatic talents are the best

the School of Nine Wishes has ever seen.

"I knew that giving you another lead role in a school musical would not help you grow as a fairy. The secret task I set you was to see if you had the talent to share your magical ability for no personal gain."

Holly nearly fainted. "So you knew I was secretly helping Polly, Winnie, Daisy and Felicity?"

Fairy Godmother nodded. "I couldn't have done it without the help of Felicity though. She began the magic that allowed you to share your drama skills with everyone."

Holly looked at Felicity. "So you knew about this all along?"

"Yes," said Felicity, looking a little sheepish.

"Thanks to you the show was a resounding success," said Fairy Godmother.

"But I ruined it!" burst out Holly. "I ruined it because I forgot a golden rule. Every part in a show is as important as any other. No matter how big or small."

"But the talent you shared with your friends saved it! It wasn't ruined in the end, and the most magical part for me was to see you want the applause not for yourself, but for your friends."

Holly beamed. "I did feel proud!" she admitted.

"And so do I," said Felicity, giving Holly an enormous hug.

Magical talent can be shared
if your heart is open enough to allow it

It's the School of Nine Wishes

trip to Sparkle Towers in

Star Surprise

Coach Commotion

Felicity Wishes was renowned in Little Blossoming for her long lie-ins. It was usual to see Felicity dashing from her house late for school each morning.

But this morning Felicity woke even before her alarm went off!

For weeks now Felicity and her fairy friends had been counting down the days until today, and finally it had arrived. It was the day of the School of Nine Wishes annual outing and the fairies were going to Sparkle Towers, the largest fairy theme park ever built.

"You're early!" said Polly in disbelief,

as Felicity landed with an un-fairylike thud beside her. Holly, Polly and Daisy were in the school car park waiting for the coach to arrive. There were excited fairies everywhere, chattering and giggling.

"Phew!" said Felicity. "I flew as fast as I could. I couldn't risk missing the coach, not today!"

"Here already?" said Daisy, looking half asleep. "That's not like you. Are you sure you haven't forgotten anything?"

"I packed my bag last night," said Felicity, rummaging around inside her bag. "Wand... pencil case... notebook... camera... keys... and... um... and..." Felicity's cheeks flushed as she rummaged a little deeper, "... and most importantly..."

Holly and Daisy leaned forward expectantly.

"Sweets!" cried Felicity as she pulled

out an enormous bag of strawberry fizzes, raspberry laces and blackberry sherbets. "You can't go on a school trip without sweets!"

Holly and Daisy cheered.

"What about your packed lunch?" asked Polly sensibly.

"Well," said Felicity, "I did think about that, but my packed lunch box wouldn't fit into this bag. And I had to bring this bag because it matches my outfit." Felicity loved to be the height of fashion at all times.

"But, Felicity, you can't eat sweets all day," exclaimed Polly. Polly desperately wanted to be a Tooth Fairy when she left the School of Nine Wishes and the importance of teeth hygiene was always at the forefront of her mind.

"Of course I can!" said Felicity. "I much prefer sweets to sandwiches anyway."

Polly couldn't believe what she was hearing. However, she didn't want to spoil the start of a magical day with a lecture so instead she made a mental note to send Felicity the latest leaflet on 'Fairy Teeth'. "Well, if you change your mind you can always share my sandwiches," she added.

The coach arrived and the class of excited fairies bundled on in a disorderly fashion.

"Quick!" said Holly, pushing her way to the front of the queue. "Let's grab the back seats!"

"Oh, no! Someone's bags are on them already!" said Felicity, disappointed.

"They're my bags, silly!" said Daisy, popping up from behind one of the seats. "I was saving them for you three."

* * *

The four fairy friends spread out

their things and made themselves comfortable on the back seat.

* * *

After Fairy Godmother had done a wand count, the coach started on its long journey to Sparkle Towers.

The trip had barely begun when Felicity, who had been too excited to eat breakfast, started feeling a little peckish.

"Sweet, anyone?" Felicity asked as she opened the enormous bag and waved it towards Holly, Polly and Daisy.

"At this time in the morning? No thanks," said Holly.

"I'm trying to give them up," said Polly. "You can't be a Tooth Fairy and eat sweets."

"Well, they're here if you change your mind," said Felicity, who happily began munching a strawberry fizz.

Suddenly the coach was filled with

Fairy Godmother's voice.

"Testing, testing 1... 2... 3..." she said into a large microphone at the front of the coach, tapping it twice with the end of her wand. "Welcome, fairies, to your annual school outing. As you know, the journey is a long one, so the teachers and I have come up with a short quiz to help pass the time. Miss Meandering will hand each of you a sheet with twenty questions. The person with the most correct answers will win a special mystery prize."

Felicity and her friends had already thought of how they'd like to pass the time on the journey, and it wouldn't leave much time for filling in a quiz!

Holly had brought her entire collection of *Fairy Girl* magazines, Polly had brought an electronic wand game to share, Daisy had brought her CD player and four sets of headphones, and Felicity had brought even more sweets!

Out of the window the scenery gradually changed as they left Little Blossoming, passed through Bloomfield, and meandered along country lanes. Most of the fairies had never been further than the outskirts of the town itself. They spent the first part of the journey with their noses pressed up against the windows in awe at the passing scenery.

Felicity and her friends whiled away the morning playing 'Friendship Wave'. Each fairy had to wave out of the back window at passing fairies and the fairy that got the most waves back was the winner. Felicity won every game because, being a very friendly fairy, she waved at everyone.

"Are you sure you don't want a sandwich, Felicity?" asked Polly, tucking into her lunch. "I thought strawberry jam sandwiches were your favourite?"

"They are," said Felicity, unwrapping another tube of sweets. "But I've got plenty more sweets and they're much yummier than jam sandwiches!"

The coach bumped along steadily and sunshine flooded in through the windows making drowsy fairies with full tummies fall into a deep sleep.

While the rest of the coach enjoyed its gentle slumber after lunch, Felicity's wings began to quiver, slowly at first but then at an uncontrollable and unstoppable speed!

"I don't feel so good," said Felicity, slowly handing back her copy of *Fairy Girl* to Holly.

"You look like you've got ants in your pants," said Polly, who had opened one eye from her snooze to see what was making the seat jiggle.

"Can I have one of your sweets?"

asked Daisy, pulling off her head-phones.

"Have them all!" said Felicity passing Daisy her bag. "I couldn't eat another sweet if I tried."

Daisy opened the bag and looked inside. "Felicity!" she squealed. "There's none left! You've eaten them all! That's why you feel sick!"

Felicity was now bouncing up and down so high on her seat that her crown kept touching the ceiling. "I can't sit still!" she said nervously.

"No wonder you've got so much energy, with all the additives in those sweets!" said Polly, eyeing up the contents list on the back of one of the packs.

Just then Fairy Godmother's voice came through the loudspeakers.

"Fairies, soon we will be stopping at a service station for petrol. It will be an ideal opportunity for you to stretch your wings for five minutes. If you do leave the coach, please return straight to your seats for a wand count before we set off."

Felicity couldn't wait to take full opportunity of the break to stretch her wings. Once outside, her friends watched in shock as Felicity flew frantically around and around, in any direction the wind took her! Felicity had never flown so fast in her entire fairy life. When she finally landed with a crash beside her friends, her wings were still quivering.

Read the rest of

Emma Thomson's

felicity Wishes®

Star Surprise

to find out if Felicity

will ever be herself again!

If you enjoyed this book, why not try another of these fantastic story collections?

1. Designer Drama

2. Star Surprise

3. Clutter Clean-out

4. Newspaper Nerves

5. Enchanted Escape

6. Whispering Wishes

8
Friends Forever

7
Sensational Secrets

9
Happy Hobbies

11
Wand Wishes

10
Party Pickle

12
Dancing Dreams

13 Spooky Sleepover

14 Fashion Fiasco

15 Pink Paradise

16 Spectacular Skies

17 Dreamy Daisy

18 Perfect Polly

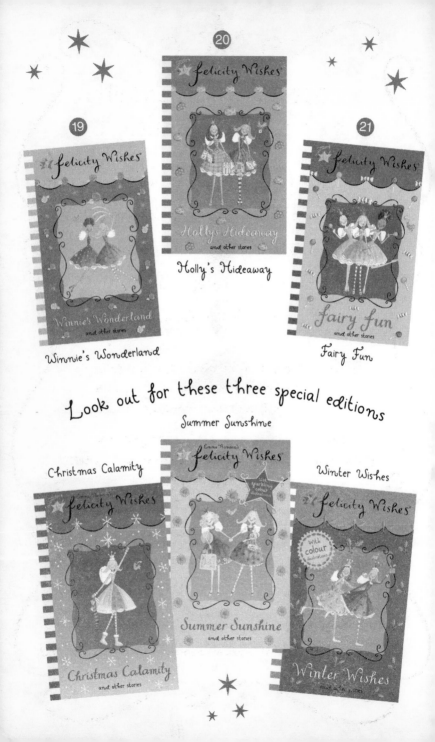

Winnie's Wonderland

Holly's Hideaway

Fairy Fun

Look out for these three special editions

Summer Sunshine

Christmas Calamity

Winter Wishes

Christmas Calamity

Summer Sunshine

Winter Wishes

SEE YOUR FRIENDSHIP LETTER HERE!

Write in and tell us all about your best friend, and you could see your letter published in one of the Felicity Wishes books.

Please send in your letter, including your name and age, with a stamped self-addressed envelope to:

Felicity Wishes Friendship Competition

Hodder Children's Books, 338 Euston Road, London NW1 3BH

Australian readers should write to...
Hachette Children's Books
Level 17/207 Kent Street, Sydney, NSW 2000, Australia

New Zealand readers should write to...
Hachette Children's Books
PO Box 100-749 North Shore Mail Centre, Auckland, New Zealand

Closing date is 30 April 2007

ALL ENTRIES MUST BE SIGNED BY A PARENT OR GUARDIAN.
TO BE ELIGIBLE ENTRANTS MUST BE UNDER 13 YEARS.

For full terms and conditions visit www.felicitywishes.net/terms

Friends of Felicity

My best friend is called Aimee,
She has a lovley personality
She is verry kind to every one but when she has to
put up a fight, I mean has to, she will.
She is a lovley friend to have and is quite funny.
Aimee has 2 dogs, 1 sister and 4 brothers. She has
browny hair and brownie, greeneyes.
She is about 1.3 metres tall.
She is a bit of an animal lover, her favorite
color is light blue. (to suit her colorings)
we have lots of fun together

we like to play:

mums + dads
dogs
babbys

(realy any thing)

From Elise McMenamin

age 7 coming up to 8 on

Year 3-4

WIN FELICITY WISHES PRIZES!

From January 2006, there will
be a Felicity Wishes fiction book
publishing each month (in Australia
and New Zealand publishing from
April 2006) with a different
sticker on each cover. Collect
all twelve stickers and stick
them on the collectors' card which
you'll find in *Dancing Dreams* or
download from www.felicitywishes.net

Send in your completed card to the relevant
address below and you'll be entered into a
grand prize draw to receive a Felicity Wishes prize.*

Felicity Wishes Collectors' Competition

Hodder Children's Books, 338 Euston Road, London NW1 3BH

Australian readers should write to...
Hachette Children's Books
Level 17/207 Kent Street, Sydney, NSW 2000, Australia

New Zealand readers should write to...
Hachette Children's Books
PO Box 100-749 North Shore Mail Centre, Auckland, New Zealand

*A draw to pick 50 winners each month
will take place from January 2007 – 30th June 2007.

For full terms and conditions visit www.felicitywishes.net/terms

WOULD YOU LIKE TO BE A FRIEND OF FELICITY?

Felicity Wishes has her very own website,
filled with lots of sparkly fairy fun and information
about Felicity Wishes and all her fairy friends.

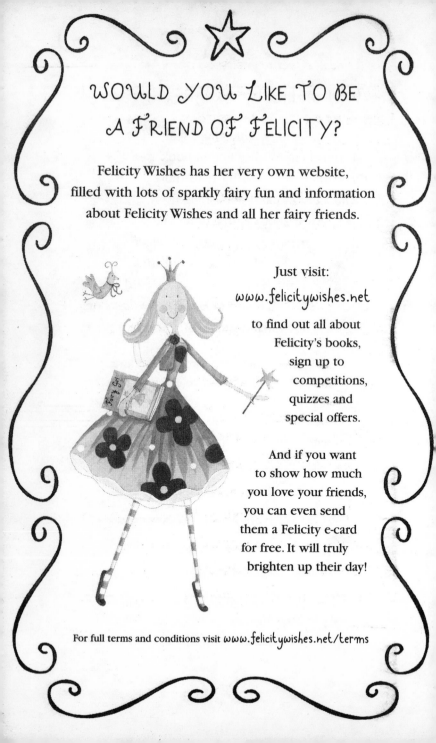

Just visit:
www.felicitywishes.net

to find out all about
Felicity's books,
sign up to
competitions,
quizzes and
special offers.

And if you want
to show how much
you love your friends,
you can even send
them a Felicity e-card
for free. It will truly
brighten up their day!